Gundog Sense and Sensibility

Wilson Stephens

Sketches by
Mary Beattie Scott

SWAN·HILL
PRESS

Copyright © 1982 Wilson Stephens

First published in the UK in 1982
by Pelham Books Ltd

This edition published 2001
by Swan Hill Press, an imprint of Airlife Publishing Ltd

British Library Cataloguing-in-Publication Data
A catalogue record for this book
is available from the British Library

ISBN 1 84037 262 1

Typeset by Phoenix Typesetting, Ilkley, West Yorkshire
Printed in England by Biddles Ltd., Guildford and King's Lynn.

Swan Hill Press
an imprint of Airlife Publishing Ltd
101 Longden Road, Shrewsbury, SY3 9EB, England
E-mail: airlife@airlifebooks.com
Website:www.airlifebooks.com

To all the spaniels and retrievers which I have bred, trained, trialled and shot over: Thanks for the memories. What they have taught me is on the pages that follow.

The author acknowledges the courtesy of Mr Derek Bingham, Editor of *The Field*, in which magazine base material, now amplified in some of the concluding chapters of this book, first appeared.

CONTENTS

OF TRUTHS UNTOLD

Often it is said of experts at gundog training, 'He (or she) has forgotten more than most of us will ever know.' This is likely to be true. To any expert, the basics of his craft become second nature. As his experience accumulates, he applies them without conscious thought. In short, he forgets them while continuing to act upon them. And he assumes that other people know them as well as he does. So when he comes to explain his techniques to those who know less than he does, it is the techniques exclusively which he passes on; he takes the nature of his raw material to be common knowledge.

Where the raw material is a living gundog, this greatly handicaps anybody who seeks to profit from the knowledge passed on in books and at training classes. At all stages – in the home or kennel, in elementary training, in advanced training, in active sport with the gun, and in competition – the prime necessity is to 'read the dog'. This means knowing what it is thinking (gundogs do indeed think), which way its inborn libido is causing it to act, what it is trying to tell its handler by its tail action and eye expression, even its hopes and fears. The classic signs of awareness, affection, fear and anger all have significance for those who can 'read' them; so do the techniques by which the human partner answers back. By each side giving intelligent responses to messages which are mutually understood, a bond of two-way confidence is built up. For those to whom experience has by slow degrees given the knack of achieving this, it is easy to leave it out of account in the belief that everybody else knows of it, too.

Quite naturally, books about gundog training are generally written by experts. Most of them suffer from this limitation. I am not an expert, and my aim is not to detail again the methods of training gundogs, or to offer variations on that theme. Others better qualified have already done this. My intention is to make more meaningful the instructions which they give by considering the dog itself, its level of perceptions, its preconceived notions, its capacity to receive communications and the means by which it best does so. These are things which I wish somebody had told me twenty years ago, when I first attempted to train seriously.

But nobody did. I had to find them out for myself, and it has been a process both rewarding and frustrating: rewarding because so much which was a mystery has been explained; frustrating because the years that the locusts eat are not restored to us, and I can never again have the good dogs which I spoiled because I did not then know what I have found out since. In passing it on, I hope a short-cut may be provided by which others may capitalise more rapidly on the instructions of the many authorities from whose writing I myself have learned so much else, and from their own observation.

It goes without saying that such an exposition of the basics can be attempted only by a non-expert who has had enough experience to learn the lessons of failure and, though infrequently, to know the sweet smell of success. I must therefore define how non-expert I am. In the past forty years I have trained seven retrievers, fifteen springer spaniels and three cockers to run in field trials, gaining 112 awards. Two have become Field Trial Champions for other people, my own competitor's level being that of amateur handlers at grass-roots.

This degree of experience and extent of success is self-evidently small compared with that of those who can claim to write from the experts' stand-point. They have taught me much. In offering now what they did not teach me I record first my gratitude, and secondly my conviction that they would have taught me even more had the fundamentals been as clear in my mind at the time of first reading as they have since become. Until we have acquired the inner secrets of human contact and canine reflex we are in the position of trying to communicate with dogs without knowing their language.

The process of training dogs to work to the gun differs from simple obedience training because the objectives are different. Obedience means that the dog is in subordination to its master, doing what it is told to do, desisting from what it is told not to do. A gundog, by contrast, is in co-operation with its master. Though both are working to the same end, for much of the time they do so independently. Instead of the man controlling the dog, the dog must have learned to control itself, and have the self-reliance to go a stage further.

Beyond this initial discipline, there lies a further dimension in the gundog's case. Situations will repeatedly arise in which the dog, out of sight of its master, must follow one possible line of action while rejecting another, sometimes more than one other. In thus exercising an option the dog must be .able to choose correctly, even though the lines of action to be rejected may be easier or more attractive than the line to be adopted, and even though what would be wrong in some circumstances will be right in others. Therefore the obedience element in gundog training must never be so repressively applied as to deny the dog freedom of action, or quench its initiative to do what is necessary without human guidance.

A simple case points the need. All gundogs must learn not to chase; what they most want to chase is rabbit if only because they know that rabbits cannot fly. Rabbits normally live under low cover such as brambles, bracken or whins in which, if a rabbit moves, a questing dog must ignore it. But if the rabbit moves far enough to break cover and be shot, the dog must follow its line when commanded, and retrieve it. If the rabbit is not dead but wounded, the dog must do this quickly enough to overtake, before it goes to ground, the rabbit which it has been taught to refrain from chasing. Despite the sequence of contradictory precepts of training which have to be bent or broken, this is all in a day's work for a spaniel.

Unlike other dogs, gundogs are thus required not merely to do the right thing, but the right thing at the right moment. This is achieved only by leaving the dog with unblunted confidence to make up its own mind when two or more courses of action are possible, and a correct choice must be made.

Even at this early stage the word 'confidence' has come into the matter. Confidence remains the dominant requirement throughout the training period and a gundog's subsequent working life. The confidence must operate in every direction: the confidence of the handler in his dog, the confidence of the dog in its handler, the confidence of the dog in itself, and (by no means easiest to build up) the confidence of the handler in his own powers. The latter is an essential pre-condition to making use of the practicalities which will be presented in this book. We cannot give confidence to the dogs we train until we have developed or simulated it in ourselves. My hope is that this process will be made less difficult by what is to come.

First, however, consider confidence in greater depth.

If a dog is to have confidence in its human partner that particular person must present himself or herself to that particular dog as a super-being, without weakness, infallible and, above all else, the most fascinating feature of any landscape into which the two venture together. It is necessary to make oneself a magnetic attraction, so that the dog's attention at all times, and its physical movements most of the time, are inclined inwards and not outwards. To do this is not a matter of 'going soft' on the dog, exciting it, talking to it, and offering it titbits; the former will establish the handler in the dog's mind only as an effusive fuss-pot and titbits will establish him as a good-time Charlie, to be welcomed but not respected. A very rare shared

11

pleasure, such as a piece of one's own sandwich at a shooting lunch, is very different; it is an act of communion, an extra binding link (if properly exploited) for the hours to come. But it should be rarely offered, so that the sense of privilege is maintained.

To make oneself magnetic is a matter of being in fact interesting; of not doing the same thing every day; of occasionally doing something unexpected without warning and without repetition; most of all, perhaps, simply being an interesting person in the dog's eyes. Dogs soon learn that such people repay watching, and focus their attention on them. Without such a directing of attention by the dog towards the human partner, the dog is not receptively inclined to take the orders which eventually come to it. And the sign that a state of receptivity has been reached is given by the dog itself, in the characteristic pose of the attentive gundog, its eyes on its handler's face.

No communication should ever be passed to a dog which is not in this position of attention. Equally, no order (even if after rebuke) should be considered properly carried out unless it is done with the tail wagging. This proves that the dog is confident of the meaning of the command given, equally confident of its ability to carry it out, is acting in partnership not in servitude, and that its handler is no bully.

We do not talk of 'dog breaking' any more, but of 'dog training' instead. Whatever we call it, the process can still be carried out heavy-handedly, and when it is the proper result cannot be attained. With gratitude I quote the words of Talbot Radcliffe, a great modern trainer, 'A dog must be healthy to be happy, and happy to be trained.' Nothing worthwhile can be achieved in the presence of reluctance and resentment.

Given that a young dog is of due age and healthy, that it will never undergo any form of instructional exercise when an adverse health factor could put it under stress (for instance, heat in a bitch), and that confidence has been attained between it and its handler, training is possible. In view of the advice which is generally given, that training should not start too early, and that the puppy should previously have had an unrestricted adolescence, its mental state at this stage needs consideration.

Some writers give the impression that the ideal state of a puppy when training begins is one of blank mind. Their readers may be forgiven for concluding that it should know nothing beyond its own desires, and have never subordinated any of these to a human will. This is an early example of experts assuming that what is taken for granted by them is common knowledge to everybody else. It is obvious that the situation thus implied is very unlikely to occur and, if it did, would place the trainer in serious difficulty.

For reasons to be stated even the elementary stages of training to the gun are likely to be counter-productive if begun before the age of eight or nine months. A gundog puppy is then an active, high-spirited, even bombastic young creature. To commence the man–dog relationship from scratch at that point would make the training process even more complex than it need be, perhaps impossible for most people. However, for the previous six months of its life, ever since it left it dam, the puppy has had to live with somebody and, within varying degrees, to be lived with. For it to have learned nothing during that period would imply a very stupid puppy or a most exceptional upbringing.

Perhaps it would be possible, at a large kennel, for puppies to be 'run on' to trainable age in a puppy house and paddock, their only human contacts being associated with food and cleanliness, leading a communal life of *laissez faire* plus *sans souci*, canine equivalents of the flower people of recent history, coming to their trainer totally green. That they would also have been developing an undue degree of pack instinct is also more than likely. But fortunately, even in large kennels, this is unlikely to happen. Life in kennel, in fact, is where the fundamental pediment for all training is based. The word 'kennel', in the context, embraces the human household if that is the puppy's domicile.

In kennel or home, a puppy learns not to be a nuisance, to go through doorways when told, to be clean, to behave at feeding time, and the other minor graces inseparable from an acceptable companion. At exercise, of which it should have enough but not too much, it will learn to 'use itself' at all paces, move with balance through cover, and the significance of that lifelong source of inspiration, its nose. It will also learn from its handler how to comply with the simple drills essential for its own safety – to know its name, to come when called, and how to walk on a lead in a composed manner. Whoever teaches it these things will notice that much repetition is necessary, and this is the reason for deferring until eight months the more serious training which involves the concentration and directing of a dog's inherent abilities, plus the implantation of new skills.

Until a puppy is about eight months old its memory has not developed the power to retain what it absorbs. It can learn and perform responses to orders which it receives several times a day – to come, to go to its kennel, and so forth. But these are repeated often enough for each repetition to restore the fading imprint of its predecessor. The exercises which are the forerunners of gun training become pointless if inculcated in this manner. Though, inevitably, most of them will have to be given more than once before they are understood, the only inculcation of real consequence is the one that lasts for life, as one of them eventually will. It is valueless to give lessons at an age when the pupil cannot be relied upon to remember them. Attempts to do so invite two adverse consequences.

In the first place, to a puppy intent on pleasing itself and so immature that the impulse to please its handler has yet to dawn, being required to sit and stay (the customary first training lesson) seems an infringement of its expected liberties. Insistence upon it establishes the trainer as an unwelcome bore, to be avoided when possible. These prejudices may become extended to all humanity, and an attitude of non-cooperation built up. Secondly, a lesson given at the age of forgetfulness presents the trainer with an insoluble dilemma when the puppy fails to carry it out a day or two later. If the trainer then insists on compliance, he may be requiring the puppy to carry out an order of which it has by then no recollection. If he does not insist, and by chance the puppy has not forgotten after all but is merely ignoring the order, he will be condoning disobedience. Either way, he would be in a stronger position had he refrained from teaching the lesson in the first place since, having done so, he cannot know which set of circumstances he is dealing with. Better to wait the extra few weeks until the age of reliable memory, after which the puppy, being then capable of remembering, can fairly be blamed for not doing so.

The dog's mind is the surface on which the trainer operates. Experiences indicates that the canine brain at its best can rise to the level of that of a reasonably bright three-year-old child, except that dogs totally lack even the limited capacity to imagine what is present in humans of that age. Dogs can, however, expect – the act of expectation being based on experience – and they possess some power of rudimentary reasoning. In addition, a large corpus of inherited aptitudes has been concentrated into the minds of gundogs by selective breeding for their special roles across hundreds of dog-generations. So, though their brains are relatively small, they contain powerful 'drives' waiting to be released and channelled towards sporting purposes.

Most of these inherited urges originate much further back in time than is generally realised, and possess proportionately greater force. The one hundred and twenty years of official pedigree records did not see the start of selective dog breeding for purposes analogous to modern shooting. That process began long before guns were invented. There is written record that six hundred years ago dogs located game birds for falconers by 'pointing' and 'setting' them, and helped the fowlers of yet earlier days by 'springing' birds into nets. There is an intriguing contemporary reference to spaniels in Wales during Norman times, and presumptive evidence that the Romans possessed the ancestors of the Italian 'braques' which were the tap-root of all gundog breeds. The desire to hunt, the sensitivity to game scent and the exhilaration which this produces, comparable to the effect of alcohol on men, have thus been refined and strengthened in every canine generation (about five years) over many centuries.

Those who did the refining, by mating the best to the best, naturally chose their favourites for this purpose, favouritism being earned by their readiness to do what was required. Thus was forged the other strand in the mettle of well-bred modern working gundogs, the compulsive wish to please those to whom they have given their hearts.

The sporting gundog of today exists for us by virtue of its internal psyche rather than for its physical presence. With its externals we are not here much concerned. An animal which is not physically efficient is useless to a sportsman; otherwise handsome is as handsome does. Its compliance with some specification of conformation, drafted in the receding past and in-terpreted with varying degrees of sense ever since, is immaterial. Our interest lies in what evolution has given us in the brain, the perceptions and the nervous system of the dog. Our aim is not to govern its bones and muscles, which would be easy, considering our superior strength and intelligence, but to influence its mind – and this can only be done by knowing the way into it.

Of whatever breed, all working gundogs share certain characteristics which vary in degree. All are athletic, energetic, resourceful, eager, sensi-tive and, so long as they respect and love us, anxious to do our bidding. Pointers and setters, which work as individuals at great distances in their private worlds of shifting air currents, cloak these qualities in a corre-sponding remoteness. Spaniels, ever at their master's side and constantly in action at his behest and in his close-up presence, have developed a vehemence in their hunting drive greater than that of the retrievers, whose skill was the last to be developed. Until the breech-loading gun made driven game shooting possible a century and a half ago, there had been no need for specialist retrievers, and the motivations from by-gone centuries, though present through their ancestry, exist in them as forces diluted by a modern requirement. The pointer-retrievers developed on the European mainland inherited a more independent tradition than the breeds developed in Britain. In all that follows, these differing emphases may affect application, though the message is valid for all.

Whatever the breed of gundog, if bred for work it will have great curiosity, a desire to search and explore, much energy, a keen sense of smell, ready recognition of game scent, and a deep-seated urge to serve and earn the

15

praise of its human partners. The problem is to concentrate these character-istics in directions which will be most useful to the dog's role, and to avoid those which run counter to it. To do this, lines of communication are obvi-ously necessary, and they are more numerous than is generally supposed.

All five senses can be used as routes into a dog's mind. At commence-ment of training they rank in descending order of importance as follows, Hearing, Smell, Sight, Touch, Taste. This order varies from stage to stage as training progresses towards the ideal culmination in which the dog would come to control itself totally, with no intervention whatever by its handler. This is obviously unattainable in practice, though we strive to get as near it as possible.

As training proceeds circumstances dictate the variations in the senses' order of importance. Sight and Smell temporarily supersede Hearing as signals convey messages previously transmitted by voice or whistle, and scent rather than appearance comes to identify the handler. Each of the five senses supplements the other four in the numerous contacts between man and dog which are necessitated not only in active sport but in daily life. In the end the fabric of the link which binds them together will be seen not as a line but as a web. In short, their unity has so many strands that a good man and a good dog work together without revealing by what means they keep in touch.

In the chapters which follow, the employment of each of the senses is analysed, the responses from the dog anticipated, and possible complications foreseen. Success in training does not consist entirely of communicating the right messages to the dog. It is equally necessary to ensure that the dog, having absorbed a message, does not misunderstand or wrongly interpret it. The process may fairly be defined as Education plus Application minus Confusion.

Part I
In Human Terms

1

INSTEAD OF SPEECH

If we analyse the inner reasons why we do what we do in training a dog, we have much more chance of correctly solving the problem of how to do it. Hence the value of reflecting on the bases from which we assert our influence, and on the influences already present in the dogs with which we deal. In offering some thoughts in this direction it is convenient to clarify a word which arises continually. For the purposes of this book the word 'trainer' means anybody, however experienced or inexperienced, who trains a gundog or aspires to; if a master of the art is specifically intended, the term 'professional trainer' will be used. The masculine pronoun will be assumed to include the feminine (e.g. 'he' means 'he or she').

When considering the characteristics of the canine mind, it is equally important to remember that we are human. Dogs have their methods of communication, dog to dog, we have ours, man to man. Both operate efficiently on their own levels, and thereby become something else which is taken for granted. So much so that we must make conscious effort to avoid falling into an elementary trap. This is the supposition (which everybody makes sometime) that our familiar communications ought to work equally well man to dog. They cannot.

Dogs do not speak English, nor any other language. Being non-linguistic, they cannot come to understand language when it is spoken to them. Their own messages are given and received among themselves by codes and signals conveyed in all five senses. Where we mainly use Hearing to absorb a message, they rely on other means than barking, growling and whining to transmit one. Nose and tongue are much used to give and obtain information. Eye signs are significant, an obvious example being as a warning. The sense of touch, in certain specialised instances, is as eloquent to them as it is to us.

In communicating man to dog it therefore falls to man's lot to teach himself the code employed by dogs, to use a version of it when possible, and when not possible to adapt his own verbal system of message-passing so that

19

a dog can understand it. We all do the latter, readily and without question, when we visit a country in which the people do not speak our own tongue. It is no wonder that we must do so when dealing with an order of Creation which is not our own. The fact remains that some people still consider a dog stupid when it does not react to words.

Our normal communication system requires re-shaping before dogs can take it in. It is necessary that we do this for more than one reason. Voice is the message-passing method which comes most easily to us, and is therefore most quickly available in emergency (there are stages of gundog training which seem to be self-contained emergencies). More importantly, it is the base medium through which all the other signals and responses are taught to a dog, and hence voice becomes the scaffolding of the training process. Just as scaffolding eventually comes down, so is voice progressively phased out when the training process successfully establishes the partnership between man and dog.

In the beginning, however, a vocal link must be evolved in a form which both sides can understand. From our side this means perpetual resistance to anthropomorphism (the ascribing of human attributes to non-humans). Words, as we understand them, being meaningless to dogs, we expect the impossible if we think they will participate in a word process, since this is essentially human; sounds are what they understand. Here the trainer's function is to relate particular sounds to particular sequels. What the words used, if any, mean to the trainer and the rest of the human race is irrelevant; what they come to mean to the dog is all that matters. To train a dog to cast itself and hunt on the command, say, of 'Sign here, please' would be very simple. The dog would find nothing odd about it.

So we can forget the niceties of expression which so deeply and unnecessarily afflict some trainers. What we must remember is the attitude of dogs to all this. Not comprehending words, being aware only of sounds, the shape of the sounds is all that concerns them. If our transmissions are tuned-in to their reception, our utterances should come over in their ears rather as the Morse code does to us, a series of dots and dashes, but varied into broad and narrow syllables.

Dogs are unaware of consonants other than sibilants and labials when the latter are projected explosively from compressed lips (the letter 'b' is fortuitously prone to emerge in this manner during training sessions). However, they are extremely aware of vowels, and of the contrasts between them. More will be said in detail on this point. Enough has been said now to indicate that speech from man to dog is non-advantageous. At best it is a contribution only to the wider system for the transference of will; at worst it is a positive hindrance to mutual understanding. The latter point is reached when speech is used to excess so that the dog, despairing of making any sense of it, takes less and less notice of it. The touch of the controlling hand – firmly, gently and reassuringly applied – says as much to a dog as anything audible.

Voice contact nevertheless looms largest in the earliest stages of man–dog relationship, long before actual training begins. Sensitivity to every form of communication constitutes about fifty per cent of the vital assessment which a trainer must make of his canine material, evidence of inborn proclivities being the other fifty per cent. The puppy which stops or turns, interrupting whatever else it is doing, at the sound of a voice (not, be it noted, a word) which it recognises has demonstrated the indispensible quality of responsiveness. If, in addition, it raises its head so that its eyes are on the human face, and thereafter holds its gaze steady, a very encouraging sign has been seen. The puppy is expecting, waiting for, even asking for his next message. A wise trainer will wait for other signs, and he will do so in a sympathetic frame of mind, considering not only the puppy's character but his own, and calculating how the two will fit. To those who, like me, train comparatively few dogs, this is a judgement of supreme importance. To stake at least two years of effort on an animal with which one has only limited hope, or no hope at all, of achieving harmony is a short cut to being disappointed by what ought to be a pleasure. The dogs alone are not to be blamed for this. We also have our idiosyncracies which do not necessarily match those of others, canine or human.

No two trainers are alike; even if their methods are identical, their personalities are not. Nor are any two dogs alike. The permutations of psychological factors are therefore limitless. Though most of us avoid using such long words to express the rough edges which are the first indicators of individuality, they do indeed exist in every case, and must be identified and allowed for. Therefore whoever embarks on training a gundog must first weigh up its character with great care.

In the process of getting to know a dog, especially when young, the prime need is to like it. But one cannot like a dog to order; one may, indeed, not like it. If a trainer, be he master or novice, does not 'take to' a dog he is well advised to act on the principle that there are other pebbles on the beach; other trainers for this particular dog; other dogs for this particular trainer. Attempting to build rapport where there is pre-existing disunity invites failure. An artist does not work on canvas which he thinks faulty, nor does a carpenter risk unsound wood. Both may be mistaken, but doubt would undermine their faith in the task. In gundog training, already presented as a matter of confidence, doubts are not to be admitted.

21

The next prime question is whether the dog is intelligent. There are signs, even at the outset of training before the power of memory is fully developed, which are of great use in estimating this. It is notable that some trains of thought, perhaps those the most deeply instinctive, can be held better than others in the early days. An eye for country is a case in point.

A cocker puppy aged six months was running free on an exercise walk. In the interests of education she was allowed to continue on the far side of pig netting for two hundred yards after crossing of her own volition at a gap, and was then whistled up. Consternation followed when she found the wire impenetrable between her and her handler. When three attempts to butt her way through it had failed she ran back – at full gallop, on her own initiative, and without encouragement – to the gap by which she had entered. Recrossing, she reached her handler breathless but triumphant. She had demonstrated an ability to notice, and to use, a detail in her environment which a less clever dog might have failed to register.

Animals with such capability in using their brains invite two comments. The first is that even the best of them are unlikely to develop their intelligence if they are constantly being spoken to, and their attention distracted from the surroundings. The second is that once the flair, and the self-reliance to use it, is developed it is permanent and grows.

The same cocker, in later life and in a different part of the country, did something else the significance of which escaped other Guns in a shooting party. At a stand in the Yorkshire dales a hare was shot by a Gun tall enough to fire over the high dry-stone dyke behind which he was placed. At the end of the drive the cocker, sent to retrieve, crossed the dyke nimbly by climbing and jumping, finding the hare without difficulty. Though well able to carry it, to return over the same obstacle would be difficult for so small a dog with so large a burden. She ran without hesitation to a gateway seventy yards to the left, came out through it, and delivered the hare without fuss. She had seen the dyke, and the gateway in it, only once before in her life. That was on a shooting day five weeks previously, on which occasion she had approached the gateway from the opposite direction. In the meantime she had worked on several other shoots. The experience of those intervening days had not prevented a memory returning to her mind at a moment when it was useful.

Such apparently inexplicable acumen is not confined to particular types of situation. A dog with brains is generally quick in acquiring the very varied aptitudes which come with experience of active work. Some are beyond human comprehension, though most of us who go shooting have experience of them. One example is the uncanny ability of some dogs to know that a bird has been pricked, even though it is flying away high and strong. Though the Gun who shot at it and, if different, the dog's handler, may be convinced that the shot missed, it is unsafe to ignore a positive indication by an experienced dog that the bird was hit.

Picking up with a flatcoated retriever bitch, in her third season, I was following the Guns to the next stand after collecting a distant runner. Realising that I could not catch up before the drive started, and wishing to avoid causing distraction, I stopped two hundred yards short of the gun line to wait until the pick-up began. With my retriever dropped, I was in a timber-extraction road through forty-year-old conifers which ran parallel to the line. During the shooting, birds planed over us. The bitch followed one hen with nose and eyes, turning to mark its line although it had looked unshot and no different from the many others during the few seconds in which it was in view. When the 'all out' whistle gave me the cue to move up, I signalled her to come. She did not move, but sat looking first to the direction in which the hen had gone, then at me, then back. Knowing her, I said, 'All right; if you're so clever, go fetch,' and checked my watch. She was away six minutes. When she returned she brought a hen pheasant, shot in the upper part of one leg.

These anecdotes are told for a purpose. Such skills as these are invaluable. But they cannot be taught; nor do I believe that they can themselves be inherited, though the aptitude for them can be. But in a dog born of working ancestors and with well-sensitised intelligence they can develop as a result of experience. This being the case, it is pointless to train a dog which does not have well-sensitised intelligence. For while the trainer is dealing with a whole host of present issues, it is the future which is the real objective; a future to which his dog of the moment is fitted more by inherited suitability than by human influence.

Therefore a fine balance must be attained between the concept of control and the development of all the natural ability with which the dog is blessed. Perhaps the best way to define this balance is in terms that enthusiasm is as important as discipline, but discipline is not less important than enthusiasm. Like so many other things, it is easier to say this than to put it into effect by the jigsaw of countless small interlocking episodes spread over a year or so which constitutes training to the gun. However, it is helpful to add one word to the equation: the reference is to 'shared' enthusiasm. If the dog sees the man as a fellow sportsman, a component of his ambitions and pleasures, he can accept necessary restraint as part of them and an easy relationship can result. But if the dog sees the man as an obstacle to his desires, a perpetual bottler-up of his heart-felt wishes, the result will be frustration. With it will come the risk of such side-effects as whining and running-in, both born of a conflict of wills.

How unity is achieved is a matter of individual touch. Some of the mechanics, however, repay a little forethought. The first and most fundamental question concerns the home background of a dog in training. Where is it to live? Account must be taken of the dog's needs and those of the human family to which it is attached.

In addition to the food, shelter and security which every dog needs, a dog with much to learn has the same need for seclusion as a human student. He must have a retreat, almost in the religious sense of the word as a refuge where he can go (or be put) to meditate in the certain knowledge that he will not be disturbed. It is in seclusion that his lessons, whether they be of casual experience or formal instruction, can sink in and permeate his mind. For this reason I have never tried to train a dog living as part of the family. I do not say this is impossible, merely that I have not done it, and see strong reasons against doing so.

During the short period in which a dog's mind most readily absorbs training, from eight to eighteen months, it is desirable not to overload the mental intake. If a dog is to be taught its job the process will not be helped if it has also to observe the social graces of house-life and be reprimanded when it fails to do so. The possibilities of this are continual.

Throughout training, and afterwards in active work, the dog should hear the harsh tone of rebuke as seldom as possible, and then only if it has itself committed some misdemeanour which deserves it. This, incidentally, is an argument which I find conclusive against taking two or more dogs out for training at the same time. Give them recreation together by all means, but not instruction, lest a sensitive dog which has committed no fault feels unjust guilt on hearing disapproval directed at a less innocent companion. A dog living in the house is open to similar injustice, but in different form. It is almost inevitable that it will be admonished for doing something that it has no cause to know is wrong; indeed, may not be wrong, merely inconvenient. Many a dog finds itself obstructing the passage of somebody carrying a tray of drinks, therefore unable to see it, and is in consequence cursed. Others are blamed for occupying a space, or a piece of furniture, where they are normally tolerated but which is temporarily required for an extra guest. The human animus may be unintentional, but this does not prevent the tone of voice confusing the dog and leaving it unhappy.

These are counter-arguments. One of the greatest of amateur handlers, the late Vincent Routledge, averred that he could not train a dog unless he could bring it into the house (a different thing, of course, from accommodating it there permanently). Moreover life among a family is the ideal 'humanisa-tion', whereby a young dog overcomes its shyness of the boss class *en masse*. I myself have found television invaluable in settling down a nervous puppy. My method is to have the puppy (many springer spaniels, particularly, go through a period of causeless fears) on my knee during a suitable programme, allowing it to concentrate its attention on the screen, stroking it while it does so, avoiding speaking to it, but carrying on normal conversation with whoever else is present. At the end of half an hour most puppies are relaxed and seem to feel themselves acclimatised into the ambience, and at ease in human company.

It may be asked, what exactly is a suitable television programme to calm the fears of a nervous puppy, while allowing human conversation to flow without protest from those who do not wish to join in? I can only say that I have found snooker and sheepdog trials ideal for the purpose. I do not believe that dogs realise the part played by one of their own species in the latter, or that it would make any difference to them if they did. The point is that both subjects involved moving objects which command a dog's attention, and neither makes enough demand on human intelligence to require silent concentration. The atmosphere is thus a living one, not the trance which is apt to surround television sets.

A balance of the factors for and against an in-house environment for a gundog, especially when being trained, underlines the need for giving it absolute privacy whenever required, less in the human interest than in the dog's. Ideally a kennel and run can be provided outside the house, but not distant from it; or a part of a garage adapted. Otherwise an area of floor on which human feet will never tread may be designated, under a sideboard being as good as any. In one family known to me each dog has its own mat, understands that it must lie on it and nowhere else, and that wherever the mat is put is the position until further notice of the dog which owns it. Whatever measure is adopted, full and positive use must be made of it – not merely because a dog should never be a nuisance, but because a dog cannot know its place if it has not got one. Its peace of mind is also at issue; a dog is greatly reassured if it feels that it has a share in the establishment, whether house or kennel, in the form of a few square feet which form its home-base.

One of the more over-estimated elements in gundog training is the idea that the way to a dog's heart is through its stomach. This may be true of dogs to whom their stomachs rank high in the priorities of their awareness, but working-bred gundogs are not like that. To them their work, the perpetual desire to hunt for game or in other ways to satisfy their curiosity about the world around them, are of much greater significance than nutritional intake.

25

They must have proper feeding, of course; no dogs need it more. But the part played by the act of feeding, and who does it, does relatively little to develop and interrupt the link between dog and handler. Of much greater concern, indeed transcending all other human interest to a gundog, is the person with whom he comes in contact with cover, scent and quarry; eventually of gunshot, flush and retrieve.

To all this the home background retains its fundamental relationship as the point of departure before adventure and of safe refuge on return. It is, or should be for the dog, the place where peace reigns and where stability is complete. It is easy unwittingly to forget the importance of this firm base for an active life, and to overlook the stresses which may disturb it is something which is always worth remembering, and questioning. To fall short in giving a gundog security invites disaster, and one is constantly reminded of ways in which this happens.

For instance, nothing would persuade me to be a professional gundog trainer, even if I were good enough. As a way of life it has great attractions. Whoever follows it does so in the presence of Nature, deep in the un-surpassed British countryside, amidst people of like mind. At first sight the prospect might seem flawless. The adverse factor is that the reputation of professional trainers, even the most eminent of them, depends less on their own skill and hard work than on the use their clients make of it. It is unfair, but true, that a trainer is judged not solely on the quality of the dogs he trains when they leave his care, but very largely on their quality after their owners have taken them shooting. Not every owner copes wisely on their first few vital days together.

A man and his dog form a team. With rare exceptions the trainer works on only half of that team, the canine half. The owner, who has fulfilled a substantial obligation in paying the bill, may be understood if he thinks that this entitles him to a dog which will do what he wants it to do when it returns to him after training. The consequence, however, cannot be unconditional. It must depend to a great extent on the home background referred to, and the insight with which the owner treats it on the dog's return from training.

If the trainer is an able one, the dog will doubtless be capable of measuring up to expectations. But it can do so if, and only if, the owner gives the same orders in the same signals and terms as the trainer gave them, and consistently observes the same conventions and procedure, for these represent to the dog reassurance and security. On this 'if' all the trainer's professional skill, and all the owner's financial investment are staked. Ideally, the trainer should train not only the dog, but the owner too. Many owners are wise enough to allow this to happen in some degree. Even then, the transition of the dog from the trainer, with whom it has spent several months, to the man for whom it is to work imposes stresses, the appreciation of which may help in seeing the dog's point of view not only in these particular circumstances, but in others too.

In the first place, the dog has come to regard the trainer's kennels and their surroundings as the norm of its world. On being transferred to a new set of surroundings all that was formerly familiar is replaced by things which are strange. Until a new familiarity is built up the dog will be in the position of a man striving to behave himself according to the conventions of a foreign country. Under the strain of doing this his responses, even to situations and demands previously encountered and long familiar, will be temporarily sub-standard.

A dog does not 'view' its surroundings from what it sees. Since sight takes a lower priority in a dog's five senses than in ours, the sense of smell becomes dominant in establishing familiarity and confidence, or doubt and alarm. Details which man takes for granted (e.g. cigar smoke or perfume) are as disquieting to a dog, even though he may eventually come to associate them with affection for a new human partner, as the exchange of fresh air for a prevailing aroma of curry would be for a man. In establishing re-assurance in face of unfamiliarity, good intentions are not enough. A dog must be given time; time to convince itself that what at first seemed strange is in truth natural; time, too, to understand the language of its new associates. While any sensible owner realises the importance of the orders it has been taught being given in the identical all-important vowels to which the dog has been accustomed, our human preoccupation with words and spelling may hide the fact that for the dog this may be much less easy than it appears to us.

Dogs cannot spell. Their reception of verbal orders is in terms, first, of voice tone, secondly of phonetics in vowel sounds. This means that accent becomes relevant. It is seldom allowed for. If the owner speaks the English of Eton and Balliol, and the trainer has been commanding it in, say, broad Scots or Yorkshire patois, the dog's ear must be given a chance to adjust to the change.

It is probable that the dog has been trained in circumstances in which the only words it heard were those which the trainer addressed to it. When taken shooting by its owner it will be required to pick out the syllables to which it is required to respond from a background of human conversation. It cannot do this until one voice has established itself first as less strange than the rest, then of paramount importance to it, so that the words it utters of concern to the dog become distinguishable from the speech surrounding it.

27

Yet dogs are taken shooting within a week, or even a day, of being collected at the end of their training. To be fair to all – to the dog itself, to the trainer's reputation, and to the owner's financial investment – a month should elapse, a month of constructive rehumanisation and build-up of understanding. Consider in greater detail what adds up to training.

2

Sensory and Extra-Sensory

Gundog training is the art of the possible. This is not a very new thing to say, but it is true in a very relevant sense. One of the limitations of its possibilities is the trainer's physique, and it is curious that while we pay great attention to the dog's physique, the human aspect is generally ignored. Obviously physical capacity affects both what we attempt and the way we achieve our desired effects.

As examples, a lady of slight build told me that she cannot pick up a full-grown retriever and shake it, as I shall advise should be done in certain eventualities; I (also slight of build) have not found difficulty in doing so. Conversely though I could run fast when young, and twenty years ago still had a turn of foot, I can now overtake an errant spaniel only in favourable circumstances. Some of us are quicker in reflex than others, more dexterous of hand. Happy would be the gundog trainer who had the speed of an Olympic sprinter, some hurdling ability, the agility of an international goal-keeper, and the rearward vision of a hare. He could use all these qualities. But none of us is built like that.

Even so, I have seen my greater contemporaries growing older, yet con-tinuing to train gundogs as successfully as ever. The late John Kent, despite being exceedingly tall, was more than a match for a springer spaniel puppy when in his nineties, his powers of arrest still effective. The reason is, of course, that we subconsciously adapt our techniques as our athleticism fades and our agility diminishes. We use our brains to save our legs, and in general rise above the handicaps which the passage of time imposes. Nevertheless, we are wise if periodically we review our tactics and methods lest, by attempting feats beyond our capability, we begin to turn gundog training into an art of the impossible. If that happens, all sorts of undesirable sequels follow, of which easily the most certain is that our dogs will make monkeys of us.

So we must evaluate ourselves intelligently. Since I can overtake an errant spaniel only in favourable circumstances, I must ensure that favourable circumstances exist wherever a training exercise is attempted in which I may need to overtake the dog. If the lady cannot pick up and shake her retriever, she must decide before the need arises what other course to adopt in gaining the same ends. Every one of us, however active, is well advised to consider, say, the relative positions of dog, handler and dummy when teaching steadiness to fall. Obviously the handler must be in a position to intercept the dog before it can reach the dummy if it 'breaks'. To make interception certain, he must ensure that he has less distance to travel than the dog. If the dummy is thrown forward over the dog, then the dog will have the shorter distance and the handler, being reduced to in-effective pursuit and admonition, will be powerless to prevent it doing exactly as it pleases. But if the dummy is thrown backwards over the handler's shoulder, and the dog breaks, the point of interception will be nearer to the handler than to the dog and, with an air of calm unhurried superiority, the handler can take appropriate action.

In cold print these may seem glimpses of the obvious. But many trainers go for years without appreciating them, and so make life unnecessarily diffi-cult for themselves. More important, such stratagems help towards the prime and essential objective that in any conflict of intentions the trainer must always emerge superior to the dog; and it is equally important that he does so in just that spirit of calm impregnability. To be angry, even to be ruffled, negates whatever exercise is being attempted, and the ripples of its adverse effect spread much wider.

Man has subjugated the horse because horses have never realised that they are larger, stronger, and capable of quicker movement than men. Had they turned their physical advantages to sensible account, they need never have become man's servants, nor performed the hard labour they were called upon to do in the centuries during which they provided the motive power for the human race. Similarly, we can bring our dogs under our bidding to the extent that they do not realise they are more nimble and elusive than we are and can, if they wish, do as they like instead of as they are told. Their minds must develop under the unbroken impression that there is no alternative to compliance with the human will when this is exercised. The establishment of this impression, in a manner which has not caused hard feelings, is an essential precursor to formal training.

Without it, the trainer has only a fractional chance of developing the results for which he hopes, as a moment's reflection will confirm. In teaching hand signals, for instance, the dog's compliance must be obtained at about twenty paces' distance. If the dog has not learned to mind its p's and q's when within reach of physical contact, the chance of this being achieved by remote control is much reduced. The simple fact is that young dogs which have learned from an early age to be considerate of their human companions, and subordinate to their wishes in small ways, will in due course be half way to complying with commands given at a distance, on much more exciting matters, and when the dog is under temptation to do otherwise.

It is also important that this ascendancy of man over dog should become established as if it were a natural fact, an inevitability, and not an imposition by higher authority achieved by conquest. It should begin as part of a puppy's earliest consciousness, being expressed in the small episodes of its daily life. My personal indicator that this process has successfully begun is a puppy which will enter its kennel when told or signalled to do so, and not leave it without permission. It is in such seemingly small matters that the ideas of the trainer's infallibility and irresistibility take root in the puppy's mind; it is also the moment when the trainer's speed of reaction and manual dexterity begin to be important. What happens?

The puppy is ordered into kennel (not the kennel as a whole, but into the part of it which is home to the puppy). Being a full-blooded ten-week-old, it has other plans and, sensing restrictions ahead, tries to dart away from the door. But I, having met puppies before, have instinctively 'read' its evasion plan, and my foot is in its way. When the puppy stops to give my foot its due glare of indignation, a practised shove puts the puppy inside the door, which is then closed. So the order has been given, it has not been repeated, and the puppy, despite private intentions to the contrary, has finished up inside the kennel; no harsh words have been spoken, nobody's feelings are hurt, confidence has not been interrupted, the puppy's self-esteem is as good as new (and of course my foot was in the right place from the start). When the same sequence has been gone through a dozen times or so, always with undiminished good humour, the puppy will come to terms with the certainty that this particular command is always followed by its finding itself in kennel, and it will thereafter not resist this apparent law of Nature.

When at first the puppy does not comply, there must be no hint of rancour or blame. At such an age recrimination is out of place. Months must pass before the puppy can be deemed to know right from wrong, and hence culpable for not doing the right thing. Friendliness must be the keynote, whichever it does. The idea of a human being, in all the pomposity of *homo sapiens*, going through the grotesque performance of bending to his will a puppy new from the nest, expresses its own absurdity. But it happens, because some people mistakenly think that this is what training consists of. Unfortunately, when it does happen, the results are lifelong and there is no remedial process. The grown dog thereafter works with an element of uncertainty in its mind, with consequent loss of pace and promptitude of action at those moments when a dog has to respond to its own initiative without the support or stimulus of its master.

The case-history of the kennel door is only one of many repetitive situations which crop up in every twenty-four hours of kennel life. Behaviour at feeding time, walking out, discipline when the handler has to open a gate or climb a fence, waiting with the rest of the group when required to do so, desisting from jumping-up, coming when called, staying within range, self-presentation for inspection, are only some of the occasions when a particular command is followed by an unvarying sequel, and for that reason comes to be complied with. In all of them man's supremacy is demonstrated – not boastfully, nor threatingly, nor in terms of superior strength, but simply as the way of the world.

The attainment of compliance in all of them depends on the man thinking and acting quickly enough never to fail in getting his own way without fuss. Anticipation is vital. Puppies with rebellion in mind move fast; their trainer must move faster. He must act on the principle that the end justifies the means. A puppy that has once out-smarted his handler will live for the rest of his life with the ambition to repeat the feat. The prevention of this happening is a no-holds-barred business, and becomes easier the more puppies one trains. The important thing is to get a hold – an ear, a leg, the skin of the back, whatever the hand makes contact with – and not let go. The techniques of a cricketer in the slips have much to commend them.

The effect (without which a professional trainer would not begin formal instruction) is that the trainer gains the puppy's full regard instead of half of it. No success in training is possible unless the trainer has his pupil's affection and, gundogs being generous in giving their hearts, only a very unusual person could fail to win it if he sincerely tried. But this would be success in only half the battle. Affection, though essential, is not in itself enough. The regard of the dog for the man must be on a two-tier level, of which the lower is affection and the higher is respect, the two being entirely compatible. The degree to which the aura of infallibility can be created by the man is the measure of the respect he can generate. In general, the chief differences between professional and amateur trainers (as classes, not as individuals) are that the professionals command respect while too many amateurs are content with affection, and professionals remember that anger does not instil respect, because respect is the opposite of fear.

Perhaps the best indication of the end-product can be seen at any field trial. Such is the rigour of the game that difficult situations occur to all competitors alike. But when professionals are in trouble the dogs they handle seem miraculously apt to get themselves out of it before crisis point is reached, so it seems to others that the professionals have all the luck. This, of course, cannot be so. By the law of averages, luck eventually equalises. What is true is that when a professional, or an amateur of professional standard, does encounter luck he recognises it and can make the best use of it. Why? Because the stronger element of respect which binds his dog to his wishes gives him a tighter tactical control, and more ready compliance. Affection generates willingness of effort, but no more.

Not everybody aspires to the competitive level, and I cite the field trial case because competition is not only the testbed but also the demonstration platform of gundog work. There, better than anywhere, can be seen what countless writers have described as an 'unfailing but invisible link between dog and handler' which it is the ambition of us all to create. To some the quoted words may have a hollow ring; most of us have said in frustration at some time or other, How nice if they were true! Yet they are no myth, and it is apparent that some men can inspire such a link while others cannot.

Further to it, I do not doubt that extra-sensory communication exists between some men and some animals. That such perceptions by animals occur in Nature for limited purposes, especially as warning systems, is quite obvious. My convictions on the point are so strong that I take them as fact, not supposition, and in corroboration offer examples in common experience.

Many fly-fishermen agree, after repeatedly experiencing a familiar sequence of events, that trout have some form of pre-awareness of imminent threat. The circumstances are that a fisherman marks down a fish which is rising to flies on the water surface. He moves into a position downstream, from which he can keep the fish in view, see which species of fly it is taking, and finally cast an artificial fly imitating that species so as to fall where the fish can see it. Meanwhile he must mount the artificial fly – he does not know at the outset which pattern it is to be – on his line. It is imperative that the fish should not know of his presence for, if it does, it will move away. If he positions himself immediately below the fish, and remains perfectly still, this will be achieved because he will be in what is to a trout a visual dead arc. Sometimes the fisherman must wait for half an hour in this position before being sure which fly he should cast. It has happened to me many times, and what follows has also occurred too often to be disregarded.

Having identified the fly which the fish is for the moment preferring, I tie it on to the nylon leader at the end of my line. I do this without movement other than that of my fingers; the rest of me, and my rod, remain motionless. An interval for observation follows. A trout seldom feeds hurriedly. It sips down each fly at leisure, then waits for a greater or less period, perhaps savouring what it has just swallowed, before re-aligning itself to watch the flowing surface for the next mouthful. To throw the artificial fly before the trout is ready is a waste of time and opportunity; the fisherman must gauge the moment when the offering will be acceptable. By careful watching, the rhythm of the fish's movements is ascertained, and the casting of the artificial fly timed to fit into them. It is when I decide that the moment for action is at hand, but before I have begun to put the decision into effect, that fish are apt to swim quietly away. They do not go with the dash of a startled trout, swift as the reflection of a swallow passing overhead, but in the manner of a prudent move consistent with the realisation that that place is no longer healthy. Yet trout feeding nearby, but for which I have not intended to aim, do not move. Repeatedly I have stood mystified, looking at the newly mounted fly and my stationary rod top, aware of the wasted effort, mystified by the departure of a fish which looked set for the next hour, wondering what I had done wrong. Other men have wondered too. Thousands agree that it happens.

The answer is not that we have been at fault; but that Nature has a warning system, and it has operated.

Similarly in the stalking of a stag there comes a moment when most preparations have been made, but no intention reached to press the trigger. The stalker and his companion are lying in the heather, having crawled into position after hours and miles of effort. The rifle has been taken from its sleeve, and checked. He who will fire it is making his final physical and mental preparations for the shot which he hopes will be as precise as a surgical operation, bringing his breathing under control and watching for the grazing beast to turn its flank and give the chance of a bullet into the heart. The moment when he raises the butt towards his cheek is notoriously that at which the stag will lift its head and trot purposefully away for no apparent reason – notorious not in cynicism, but from accumulated experience.

Hooking a trout and stalking a stag differ from most other sporting moments of truth because in both cases the quarry is totally unaware of a human presence. If it had become aware, the trout or the stag would not have remained there. They have had none of the forewarning provided by hounds hunting, or by a questing dog, or a line of beaters. Yet trout and stag, plainly not knowing of the proximity of intruding man, both seem to become aware of a developing menace, the awareness becoming positive at the moment when the menace is passing from the preparatory stage into that of being actual. For me, there is no doubt that an extra-sensory transition has taken effect, and that these creatures have been alerted not specifically to Man, but to danger in general.

If this can happen to wild species, it does not seem impossible that a similar transition of awareness can take place between Man and the immensely more intelligent and sensitised dog. And between these two, after their epochs of interdependence and domestication, such a transition could well have been extended to other matters than awareness of danger.

Assuming such perception to be a fact, the practical question is whether it can be projected at will. To a limited degree, I believe this to be possible. When exercising dogs in a group occasions often arise in which one of them runs on too far ahead. When several dogs are out together it is wise to keep commands to a minimum lest non-offenders find themselves in the position of hearing orders with which they need not comply, which is one step towards allowing them to choose which orders to obey. One is therefore slow to make a recall. Frequently I have found that when eventually I decide to whistle or call, the dog in question will turn of its own volition and fall back to a proper position in the party before I can put the decision into effect; performing the action with a promptitude which would have pleased me had I in fact given the order. Trainers more gifted than I may well be able to develop and use this mind-to-mind influence, developing it to cover less elementary situations.

We more ordinary mortals can only admit to ourselves the probability that such a thought-transference process occurs, and remember that, if it does, it almost certainly works both ways. Hence (to quote again the test-bed function of field trials) the handler who expects his dog to run-in is likely to see it do so within a few minutes; but the handler who thinks that his dog will do no such thing is unlikely to be parted from it. The conclusion is that, since the drift of our thoughts may be intercepted by our dogs, they should be fit for our dogs to share. We must be of good cheer, so that the dogs we are training will be likewise; confident, so that the dogs will continue to think of us as capable of coping with any situation, and particularly with disobedience by them; and equable, so that even in moments of guilty conscience (dogs do indeed have consciences) they will not be afraid of us; friendly towards them, so that they will turn their eyes to us frequently as we share experiences.

These are the attributes of ourselves which we must have established in the minds of our trainee dogs by the time they are nine months old. That is the end of the age of innocence, the beginning of the age of formal education. The giver and the receiver of the training process have thus established their different positions, and formed their estimates of each other's character. Because it is a dividing point between raw material and the inception of a finished product, nine months old is a stage of great importance in a dog's life. Let us now assess the position from the two sides.

The puppy has all its future before it, and all its ancestry behind it. Generations of selective breeding have concentrated in it great stores of energy, waiting to be released in the ways which its forefathers followed. The puppy, of course, does not at this stage know what these ways are. But unless it is very unlucky it will have already felt that tingle of excitement which results from occasional touches of smell in field or lane, setting its tail going, and producing that heightened activity amounting to a mild euphoria which is the foretaste of new worlds ahead. But otherwise its mind is filled with trivia, the petty obsessions of puppyhood such as slippers, cats, food and the urgent necessity of making friends with every stranger who happens along. He does not know the most obvious thing that we know about him; that he is, for instance, a retriever and that recovery will be his mission in life, or a spaniel dedicated to searching in face of every natural difficulty, or a bird dog whose destiny is in the wind instead of on the ground, or a pointer-retriever with his own particular combination of these vocations. As the age of innocence ends, all gundogs are simply puppies.

The trainer knows very well all the things the puppies do not. He has information, experience, imagination, and ambitions to be realised. In his mind is a very clear picture of what he hopes the puppy will become when fully grown. But if he is wise this is a hope only, not an expectation, still less an all-obliterating aim. The greatest trainers of all time have never been able to do more than bring their dogs to the optimum peak of their natural ability.

Ability is inherited. It cannot be grafted into a dog by human agency. A dog's maximum potential is not decided during training; it was decided by the fusion of the genes on the day its sire and dam copulated. All that the human race can do is to give that potential every chance to develop and – more important because there are so many ways in which it can happen – to avoid stunting it by unwise training or misunderstanding. The trainer has means of entry into the dog's mind, he knows its limitations, and the mechanics of its communications system (or, if he does not, he will soon find out).

The way is now clear for the dog and the man to begin their partnership. The initiative is with the man. He must not lose it. And he must remember throughout the long, complex and sometimes contradictory process ahead that it is important to recognise clearly the reason for each of its many separate steps because we each have our own individual style and must never forget that in the quest for success what counts is 'not what you do, but the way that you do it'.

3

BY VOICE ALONE

Here the message system is governed by 'not what you say, but the way that you say it'. Since the vocal medium, man to dog, is not words but sounds, the degrees of meaning must be separated from each other by something other than the syntax which governs human speech. Tone fulfils this function. It is of all-transcending importance in communicating with dogs. They are susceptible to its smallest nuances, including those not intended. When it is said that a trainer must control himself before he can control his dog, than which nothing is more true, three-quarters of the meaning is that he must control his voice. More will be conveyed by its pitch and timbre than by the most carefully thought out combinations of syllables and vowel sounds.

Failure to think out the use of the voice is productive of many difficulties. In the first place, how much voice should be used? The answer is as little as possible – in terms of both volume and frequency. Gundogs (indeed, any dogs) should be spoken-to quietly. There is no mystic reason for this, but a very practical one which a moment's consideration will make clear. Those who habitually address their dogs in a parade ground roar leave themselves little room for extra emphasis. Since they are already splitting the ear-drums of all and sundry, there is no way by which they can increase the impact in emergency. Furthermore the dog that is always addressed fortissimo will ignore loud commands as readily as any. The strength of voice used should be rather less than the minimum estimated to be audible by the dog at whatever range it happens to be. Dogs have better hearing than we have, until deafness supervenes with old age.

Nothing is gained by making it easier for a dog to hear its orders. If a dog is not responding, the voice should be lowered, not raised. The dog will then listen more carefully, for fear of failing to hear something to its advantage – provided, of course, that it thinks the handler interesting enough to be given continued attention. This sequence of action and reaction can be turned to good account by any trainer with a dog which lets its concentration wander

(I have yet to meet the dog that did not). All that is needed is to use an especially quiet voice for the orders which the dog most wishes to hear; to come out for exercise, to go for a retrieve, to flush a rabbit known to be in a particular seat, to come for its food, for examples.

This does not mean that a loud voice should be used for the orders which the dog least wishes to hear. Far from it. A loud voice should not be used at all, it being almost invariably counter-productive except in one urgent circumstance. If it is never used at other times, a loud voice can by virtue of its surprise-factor be invaluable in saving a dog from danger by attracting its attention. A running pheasant, having been hunted into and along a hedgerow crosses a lane ahead of an approaching car. A loud shout can break a questing dog's contact with the line so that an immediate, quieter command to drop can save it from running under the car.

The counter-productive effect of voice used loudly results from it being so often a medium for the user's frustration and anger. Who has not heard the decibels build up as some increasingly irate sportsman tries to call in a dog which is evidently enjoying itself on an enterprise which is evidently untimely, illegal, or both. The tones which began by being merely virile mount through the stentorian to the crescendo, and from menace towards rage. Still the dog does not return. No need to wonder why.

When the first 'Come in' was barked out the dog had better things to do (in its own opinion). So absorbing were these matters that its repetition was likewise ignored. Louder yet and louder came the subsequent summonses, with an increasing element of anger, which becomes more difficult to conceal as the voice is raised. At that stage a dog can be understood if it concludes that in his present mood its master may not prove an agreeable companion, and is best left to cool down for a bit. The voice, in short, instead of attracting the dog as the handler intended, has increased to a degree which repelled it. The louder the initial commands, the sooner this situation will be reached; the softer, the less likely that it will be reached at all.

A soft tone, in addition, is more easily kept level. Gundogs, long bred for 'biddability', which is short for readiness to absorb a message, seldom need the higher-pitched wheedling tones seemingly required to convince other breeds that they are being addressed. Though sometimes needed to gain the confidence of a difficult puppy, these should be discontinued as soon as possible. If excessively used, they have the effect of stirring up and exciting a dog which, believing that its human companion is playing the fool, proceeds to do likewise. If a dog is to become sensible, and remain so, the voice it hears must be sensible, too. A gundog cannot be a purposeful worker and simultaneously play that role of court-jester which is expected of many a family dog.

A trainer greatly eases his task if he consciously practises the use of his voice, drilling himself so that suddenly developing problems will not disturb his control of it. Indeed, his voice in many ways equates with a horseman's hands; both should be calm and steady. Just as fidgeting upsets a horse, nagging unsettles a dog.

Having considered the nature of voice, man to dog, the obvious sequel is to consider what it should say. Here we encounter that combined watershed and litmus test of the man–dog relationship, the dog's name. The human attitude to it is a great give-away. Nothing more readily reveals a non-sophisticate than the question, when meeting a dog for the first time, 'What's his name?' It does not matter. The name is insignificant, one of the least important things about a dog, even to the dog itself. Those who set great store by knowing it, reveal that they know very little else.

A dog must, of course, have a name; but for two reasons only. First, to identify it when referred to in conversation or writing; secondly to enable it to be called from a group of other dogs to the exclusion of the rest, which is what huntsmen, when they want a single hound from a pack of twenty couple, call 'drawing'. A dog does not require to be identified in its own mind, so its name is to itself of limited importance only and, if properly trained and handled, it will seldom hear it except in this particular circumstance.

The late Major Hugh Peacock, a master of the art of the dog, found that the names of his dogs came less readily to his mind as the years mounted. As he generally had up to twenty in his kennel, this might have presented a problem. He solved it by calling all of them simply by the word, 'Dog'. When he uttered it, only the one he wanted obeyed. At first I suspected bluff, and used to have bets with him on the principle of nomination shots at billiards. This grew expensive since he always won. The secret was, of course, that his dogs constantly looked at his face. Therefore he could catch the eye of the one he wanted, which would then know that it was being spoken to. The others, not having had their eyes caught, knew that for the time being they were not being addressed. It was a useful example that the man–dog link, when fully developed, is made to be dependent on more than one sense, in this case sight as well as hearing.

However limited their use, gundogs' names must be properly chosen. Whether they are agreeable for a man to utter is one calculation; whether they are ear-worthy for a dog to recognise is another. The proper choice is more insistent to the dog's hearing than a bright colour-pattern would be noticeable to its eye. Dogs being little aware of consonants, other than sibilants, our words are to them what Chinese surnames are to other races – sequences of vowel sounds. A dog's name consisting of only one vowel sound should be avoided as it will not be easily distinguished from the other words which its owner uses; nor will a repetition of the same vowel be so distinctive as two that are different.

To be most readily intelligible to a dog, a name must have at least two syllables. Hence many gundogs are called Whisky or Sherry, but very few Port or Gin. The connotations are equally inspiring, but the former two names are readily answered while the latter two are not. These examples demonstrate a further weakness. To be fully effective, the vowel sounds in di-syllabic names should contrast more strongly than those quoted, as in Ru-by or Si-mon. Given contrast in vowel sequence, two syllables are enough to provide non-confusable permutations for three or four gundogs in a household. Huntsmen, with ten times as many names to find, for long insisted on three syllables. This led to the euphony of English hound names which is one of the minor beauties of the hunting field.

Once the significance of vowels, and the non-significance of consonants in man–dog linguistics is appreciated, the hazard becomes apparent of choosing a name, the vowels in which, to the canine ear, are also those of a word of command. Thus there are various grids through which a proposed name must be tested for vowel-value. Are the sounds sufficiently different from each other? Are they capable of confusion with those already allotted to another dog in the kennel? Do they, when dissociated from their consonants, resemble an established word of command for which they might be mistaken in the heat of a moment? Having now named about a hundred dogs, experience has taught me that only a limited number of names are 'safe' for gundogs, which explains why they consequently recur. To take an innocent example, there will always be a Trigger, a Wigeon, and a Brandy.

Having chosen a name, the next consideration is the use and mis-use to which it may be put. Over-reliance on the name is the source of many difficulties which fade away when the place of the name in man–dog communication is seen in its true perspective. To a dog which is not taken seriously, his name is the word he will hear most often throughout his life; so often indeed that the time when he will take no notice of it is unlikely to be long delayed. A trained dog hears his name only in exceptional circumstances.

His name will not be used, for instance, as if it were a summons to approach. For that purpose a whistle is preferable; it is less obtrusive to nearby humans, more imperative, and carries further. At close quarters a click of the tongue has the same effect. Those who rely on the reiteration of the name in calling up their dogs provide an object lesson in faulty man–dog technique.

The situation is familiar, on a shoot, on a walk, anywhere. A dog is missing. Its owner is calling its name in an effort to re-establish contact. His voice registers in turn impatience, anxiety, irritation, beguilement, false optimism, despair – all the gamut of feelings which all of us have had in those circumstances. But what of the dog's feelings? It has evidently found something to command its interest which for the moment outweighs its interest in the handler, than whom the dog is in a much more enviable position. The handler does not know where the dog is, and is consequently worried; the dog cannot fail to know where the handler is, so has not a care in the world. When he has finished whatever he is doing, he has only to go to wherever the voice is coming from, and join up with his *alter ego*, his sense of security unimpaired. By continually advertising his location, the handler has surrendered even his rarity value.

He has made three errors – two serious, one gross. He has used the dog's name too much; he has used his own voice too much; worst of all, he has accepted for himself the duty of maintaining contact with the dog, instead of establishing it as the dog's duty to maintain contact with him. When once this elementary point is settled the man–dog relationship begins to take on a new and saner character, saner at least from the human viewpoint. For the man is not the servant of the dog, as he has allowed himself to become in this instance. The dog should be the servant of the man, in small things as in great, as much in off-duty moments as when working to the gun. The causes and the remedies analyse themselves quite simply.

My friends sometimes ask me, rather flatteringly, why my dogs 'always come first time' when called. This is something of an exaggeration; they do not 'always' come first time; I wish they did. But perhaps they come first time more often than some of the other dogs in the village, and to this extent the short answer to the question is that they come first time because I do not call them a second time. If, when they are out of my sight, or out of their permitted range, they are called up it is their job to find me; it is not my job to find them, nor to constitute myself a kind of homing beacon, guiding them in by sonic signals. They are 'called' in not by voice, but by whistle, the use of the name having been avoided after early puppyhood. Again, the perspective must be reversed, and the matter appreciated from the dog's side, to reveal the full truth of the matter.

If the use of the dog's name is overworked, by being employed for purposes other than its function already stipulated, its only effect is to interrupt the dog's concentration. To the dog, the concept of a name as a specific title applicable only to itself, is impossible to grasp. It accepts it merely as another sound pattern, albeit a familiar one. In time it arouses its attention and its affection, not because of itself but because of the tones in which it is sometimes uttered. When used out of context the dog finds it can ignore it without loss.

If, in early training, it had been given the impression that it would indeed be its own loss if it did not keep its eye on its trainer, the dog would have grown up in the belief that its trainer (or subsequent master) needed watching, and could not be relied upon to be where expected if left to his own devices for too long. Because of the age of early training, eight to eighteen months, such an impression would have gone deep enough to last for life. Its effect would have been to change the direction of the dog's attention from outward to inward, flowing from the perimeter of its active radius towards its handler as the magnet in the centre. Without such early indoctrination of inward flow, the dog is at liberty to regard the world as its oyster, through which the handler's destiny is to follow, acting as an omnipresent help in trouble, and at other times condemned to a low profile.

To establish inward flow, some simple ploys can be put into effect while the dog is young enough to be impressed by them. It is obvious that no clear distinction can be drawn between right and wrong until the dog has acted each way, and brought the consequence of doing wrong on its own head – if possible without human intervention. In the present instance there is no point in exercising a young dog in a routine manner, the handler announcing his continued presence by voice or whistle whenever the creature goes out of sight. What is needed is imagination, opportunism, a lack of self-consciousness, and waterproof clothing.

If the puppy is allowed freedom to behave precisely as it likes in surroundings of safety, three desirable effects will follow. It will learn boldness and enterprise; it will develop its style and movement; and it will get itself lost. It does not have to go far to do the latter, just far enough to be aware of having broken contact with its handler. He, having learned wisdom, will then promptly vanish, maintain total silence, and let the puppy find him.

How to vanish presents few problems, apart from appreciation of the fact that the puppy will not be looking for his master, but smelling for him. In long grass, bracken or heather, merely lie flat – ignoring the surprise of passers-by who have a knack of turning up at such moments. Where there are trees, step behind one, downwind of the dog. The proviso may seem superfluous. It is a fact, however, that many people training dogs are more often aware of the time of day, which does not matter, than of the set of the wind, which matters very much. Sometimes, though not often, the reactions of the puppy can then be watched, and they are good value.

Surprisingly soon, the puppy will be looking eagerly round for company; then eagerness will be superseded by anxiety. An agitated search will begin, and when it ends the tail-wagging and the licking will be graphic evidence of the puppy's relief. If its name had been called, or a whistle blown, it might have continued disobeying to its heart's content. But silence cannot be disobeyed, nor separation ignored. If this minor stratagem is repeated a time or two, the puppy will keep its eyes on the handler as a routine precaution, never knowing when he will disappear. In most cases one is kept under such close surveillance that the vanishing act ceases to be possible.

When the puppy finds me, I make a point of not speaking, but give it a pat or some other indication of approval. I do not otherwise move for perhaps five minutes. I let the puppy come as close to me as it wishes. This is generally very close. Sometimes I allow it to put its nose up the sleeve of my jacket, a trick I was taught in boyhood by my grandfather. Puppies will sometimes remain so for several minutes on end, quite motionless, evidently in great contentment. I believe the bond between us is thereby strengthened.

It may be asked what happens if the puppy does not seek out its trainer, but pursues its own affairs or, as has twice happened in my experience, merely goes home. In the former case the trainer has not made himself sufficiently interesting to be essential to the puppy, for whom the landscape does not seem empty without him, as it should; he has some more self-projection to do. In the latter case the same applies, with the added deduction that this is a nervous puppy requiring a build-up of confidence by being allowed free running on unfamiliar ground.

This exercise exemplifies how the effect of the voice can be enhanced by withholding it, leading the dog to desire what it has not got – indication of the trainer's whereabouts and continued goodwill. As in all else, that which is in abundant supply eventually becomes devalued. The less voice is used, the more notice will be taken of it; the more it is used, the less effect it will have. Constantly uttering a dog's name for no purpose perceptible to the dog leads the dog eventually to treat it as meaningless, and there can be no surprise at this. Repeating 'Hi-lost, hi-lost' to a dog which is already doing its best not only breaks its concentration, turning its senses away from the scents it is trying to unravel, but has the long-term effect of decreasing the attention which it will subsequently pay to verbal commands in general.

This raises the question of what the verbal commands should be. Believing as I do that they should be as few as possible, I was surprised to find that I regularly use twelve of them. From the list below it will be seen that there are only two monosyllables, that in no case are the vowel sequences identical, and that the vowel contrasts are sharply defined. What the various expressions come to mean to dogs is much wider than what the words signify to us. Here is my canine vocabulary, with applications and comments:

1.   *Hup*: To drop, invaluable as the basis of all verbal discipline. It can be uttered with equal promptitude whether the trainer is breathing in or breathing out (a time factor which may seem trivial but can be vital). The only consonant, an emphatic labial, comes at the end.

2.   *Heel*: Walk at attention. Though monosyllabic its vowel-shape is distinctive.

3.   *Come in*: Approach me. If I wish the dog to continue the approach until it rejoins me, I slap my leg.

4.   *Go fetch*: The executive order for going out to make a retrieve.

5.   *Go back*: Move further out, the direction being indicated by hand signal.

6.   *Over*: Cross whatever obstacle confronts the dog – fence, hedge, wire, river, etc. It does not necessarily mean surmount, since some obstacles will be better traversed under or through.

7.   *Up in*: Enter kennel, vehicle, train, boat, etc., whether this involves jumping or not.

8.   *Gently*: Calm down, whether for rioting dogs in kennel, or for an over-excited beginner picking up game.

9.   *Gone away*: Carry on with whatever has been ordered. It does not merely indicate that game previously present has departed, but signifies that whatever interruption has occurred – empty haunt found, pause while Gun reloads, etc. – is ended and activity can be resumed.

45

10.   *Leave alone*: Desist. Not merely from picking up long dead mole, etc., but discontinue any other superfluous or undisciplined activity. I do not use 'No!' for this purpose, because I find it ineffective unless said loudly. The triple vowels are more emphatic.

11.   *That'll do*: Cease activity. An excellent expression borrowed from sheepdog trials, and useful as a 'stand down', indicating that the dog is no longer under orders for the time being.

12.   *Good dog*: Free to act as it pleases, as when allowed to go to its food bowl.

The way in which the concept of sounds instead of words extends the range of meanings is apparent. With variations imposed by inflexions of the voice, and the scope of an intelligent dog's interpretation according to circumstance, a very adequate vocal language is encompassed by these twelve phrases. We must continue to think of them as sounds, not as verbal formulae. If we tie ourselves or our dogs down to their literal gravamen, we are in trouble. Words can be a barrier rather than an aid to communication. The heart-felt dictum of King Lear, 'Zounds, I was never so bethumped with words since first I called my brother's father dad', could be echoed by every gundog trainer, and by all gundogs if they could speak. Words complicate simple issues until we are more likely to deceive ourselves than to deceive our dogs.

A clear case of this is presented by the simple command 'Heel', quoted above. The word itself is one of the fetishes of the man–dog relationship. As a command, it is one of the most frequently disobeyed, even though it is very seldom literally intended. It has entered the idiom of the English language in the sense of meaning the establishment or recognition of dominance. Yet who wants a dog to come to heel, especially a gundog? For sporting purposes a dog at heel is in a pointless and undesirable position. Nobody with a clear idea of what he is about would dream of training dogs to walk there. In some cases the problem is to teach them not to.

Consider the facts. What is meant when the order 'Heel' is given is that the dog should fall-in beside its handler in a position where (a) it is under control, (b) it can take an intelligent interest in surrounding events, (c) the handler can see it. If we said what we mean on such occasions the command would be not 'Heel' but 'Knee'. Since dogs recognise vowel sounds rather than consonants, the choice of word is immaterial to them. It is obvious, from the large number of dogs which walk sensibly beside their human partners, that imprecision in anatomical allusion has not always affected training. However, some people do allow the wording, so to speak, to mislead them as to the objective.

A dog which is actually at heel is behind its handler. It is impossible to imagine a less helpful place for it. While shooting is actually taking place, or is immediately anticipated, a retrieving gundog must be in a position to mark the fall of whatever is shot. If the fall is in front, as it is more often than not, most of the view will be invisible to it if literally at heel – hidden in the dead arc subtended by the dog's master. He, in his turn, may wish for occasional re-assurance that his dog is still with him. If the dog is behind him, he cannot see it; unless, that is, he turns round and looks for it, thus risking buying himself six feet of ground by tripping and falling.

What is worse is that the dog has two good reasons for knowing that if so placed, he is out of his handler's sight. The first is that there is no substitute for intervisibility in maintaining that control which is based on the dog's subconscious feeling that he is in the man's thoughts – the beginning of the extra-sensory influence whereby practice enables the best handlers to maintain the so-called 'invisible link' between themselves and their dogs. The second, sad to say, is experience all too easily acquired.

When, say, four or five dogs are exercised together one can almost see it happening. Dog personalities are as variable as human, and from their revelation much can be learned. Whether in a group of gundogs or in a pack of hounds, the characters sort themselves out.

One or two will jostle for position as close as possible to the human pack leader, like schoolchildren for whom walking next to teacher is a status symbol, and thus come naturally towards the knee. Among the rest the softies, goody-goody by nature, will be in sight at least intermittently. But almost always ones, generally potentially the best worker, elects himself or herself to the blind zone at heel which the handler cannot see unless he contorts himself, or is eccentric enough to carry a rear-vision mirror. From this unobservable station a dog can exercise all his unofficial initiative, slipping off into bramble or bracken to push up a pheasant, or to peg a rabbit from its seat; falling out for thirty yards or so to pick up especially luscious couch tips, if not something quite unspeakable; popping up from time to time, looking irritatingly virtuous, to press unwanted and squirming moles or verminous hedgehogs into his master's hand.

Two of my dogs lived most of their lives in that blind zone which alone merits the definition 'heel'. It seems to be much envied, for I have noticed that when, for one reason or another, its normal occupant leaves the kennel, a successor promptly takes it over as his own. The process of re-converting a self-appointed 'heeler' into a civilised 'knee-er' is not always possible except when the dog in question is taken out alone. But the practice of walking to knee is not initially difficult to inculcate. As has been said, it comes naturally. This is not surprising, since being positioned thus must be much more interesting for the dog. It also enables the handler to maintain vigilance without difficulty and, by being forewarned, to prevent 'breaks'. Moreover these are less likely when a trained dog can see all that goes on, than they are when the same dog wishes to see but cannot. For me, the ideal is a retriever or spaniel which walks beside me with its withers aligned on my knee. That is hardly what 'Heel' implies. The important thing is to know the general effect which we hope to inculcate, and not to be blinded by the terminology.

Equally important in the transmission of messages is the part played by voice in adapting the shape of the dog's thoughts to meet the needs of the moment. This is an altogether more subtle process, instinctive to some men, but not to others. A countryman, well accustomed to livestock, probably acquires the knack, by imitating his seniors, so young that, if he thinks of it at all, he assumes he was born with it. But to those whose life style has accustomed them to dealing with men rather than beasts, and hence in words rather than sounds, the full use of the quality of the voice does not often come naturally. It has paid me to go to the trouble of practising it.

It is over-simplifying to say that the technique is to use a tone to fit the mood, though this in itself is true. There are obviously different intonations to convey command, reminder, admiration, congratulation, caution, encouragement, reproof, disappointment, contempt. But they can be put over effectively or ineffectively.

Effect is gained by keeping the level of the voice low – 'making the dog listen for it' is a good description. The volume band within which all these intonations can be (and should be) conveyed is surprisingly narrow, the perceptions of a working-bred gundog being so extremely sensitive in this respect. I have been amazed at how small a difference can produce so positive an effect. There is therefore no need to be histrionic about it. Ham-acting is counter-productive.

Reproof does not require the gravel-voice of an outraged drill sergeant; indeed too savage a cadence is capable of so disturbing a conscientious but timorous dog that it will make no sense for some minutes afterwards, in extreme cases some hours. Generally it is enough for the trainer sincerely to feel the reaction to be conveyed; his voice will then do the job for him. The advantage of practice is that it enables the trainer to monitor his own performance, to realise his range of possibilities, and sometimes to experiment in producing effects.

The latter, of course, is something which one would not wish to do other than sparingly, for fear of confusing a dog. I occasionally come near to doing it when dealing with a wayward puppy to whom it is necessary to give lessons in the basic matter of just paying attention to me. But my conviction was finalised many years ago when I put a retriever bitch on the drop and then tried to produce a predetermined series of psychological reactions in her without using any vowel-syllable combinations she would recognise. She registered the drooping ears of contrition, the raised head of eagerness, the thumping tail of anticipating, the alert eye of co-operation all in sequence and several times repeated in response to my quietly reciting *The Ancient Mariner* with appropriate variations in tone.

In practice, some thought must be given to the words used, even though it is recognised that the tone alone will convey the intended message to the dog. After years of reflection I have come to the conclusion that the sensible course is to say whatever comes into one's head, but to keep it short, and think only of the tone. The dog will not understand the words anyway, and the uttering of these most appropriate to the occasion is a positive help towards pitching the voice suitably. A colourful example might be some glaring and premeditated offence by the dog. In this case something equating to what Sir Winston Churchill once described as 'observations of a general character, mostly beginning with the earlier letters of the alphabet' greatly assists in conveying the appropriate strength of feeling. But no matter how provoked, I have also learned to refrain from anger whenever possible, though doubtless I still do not refrain often enough. Anger is a form of violence, even if psychological violence only and, because it is alarming, violence disturbs the mind of any animal, leaving it unable to draw a helpful conclusion from the cause and consequence of its actions. I believe contempt, easily expressed by tone, is the most extreme form of disapprobation to yield desirable results.

To apply tone-consciousness to actual working or behavioural situations requires one other element, the vital one of timing. Just as a wrongly timed order to troops marching on a parade ground can cause a whole platoon to trip and stumble, so a properly timed order or signal to a questing gundog can achieve a crisp, instant response instead of a delayed, untidy one. It is a matter of experience, insight, and practice – none of which can be put into effect unless it is known that the need exists.

Voice, the skilful use of which requires appreciation both of its limits and its possibilities which so far transcend speech, is the first medium by which the trainer's mind can make contact with the dog's mind. As will be seen, physical contacts can be made with great advantage in addition, but they cannot do what voice can do. By voice the dog can be told those things which will later be conveyed by whistle or signal, or not conveyed at all because it will have made them its second nature. So (as with much else in gundog training) what the dog has learned is very soon superseded, in this case by contacts and systems involving other senses than voice and hearing.

4

EYE TO EYE

Of the many mysteries of evolution, the eye is among the most enigmatic. Essentially it is merely the organ by which creatures make themselves aware of their surroundings through the sense which we know as sight. But the eye alone is not sufficient to provide full vision, which is why this faculty is possessed only by the higher (most fully evolved) orders of Creation. Many of the lower (least evolved) orders have no eyes at all; those a little further up the scale have eyes which distinguish between light and darkness, but no more; only the highest orders, which include humanity and dogs, can form a view in perspective and movement, and assess what it means. The process of view-interpretation in detail is not performed by the eyes, which merely pick up and pass on the evidence, but in the brain. The process is presumed to be a low-tier form of imagination, perhaps the reflex version of the constructive imagination of which Man alone is fully capable.

Eyes are thus organs evolved for the reception and analysis of light and its reflections. They consist of the same tissues and liquids as the rest of the body, and are operated by photoreaction in accordance with laws of physics which are themselves inanimate. They are purely functional, serving needs which evolution has brought about in the interests of survival. That is the unarguable purpose and performance of the eyes, which would be well discharged if there were no more to be said.

But, for reasons unaccountable by science, there is more to be said. The eye is one of the main routes by which one being can convey messages into the brain of another, or derive messages out of it – whether the other wishes it or not. Human to human, examples are boundless. By looking into the eyes of others we can share love, hate, fear, amusement and almost any other combination of feelings. So too can non-human mammals in their degree; if we look closely, we can see them doing so. In the case of those which we know well, generically or individually, we can to some extent read their thoughts, and in such cases as the dog and the horse we do so as a matter of course.

They, too, can read ours. They do so more often than we think until events direct our attention to this, another undefined quantity in the world closely around us. Since the revelations and receptions by the eye are involuntary we cannot avoid them, nor in any significant way can we control them. Here we again approach the frontiers of the extra-sensory, but this time we are on ground so solid as to permit no doubt or argument. The eye has physical and psychological implications which are important in gundog training, and if ignored leave a considerable gap in a trainer's mental equipment, and in his defences against failure.

If we cannot look another man in the eye our contact with him is both limited and suspect. If he cannot look us in the eye when there is no physical obstacle to his doing so, we rightly draw unfavourable conclusions. The expressions which flow back and forward through the eyes are formidable. When we wish to gauge another man's reactions in a situation of maximum stress, it is at his eyes that we look – not at his hands to see if he is clenching his fists, nor at his mouth to see if he is compressing his lips in rage.

Through our eyes and into the eyes of others, we exert will-power. Man to man, we sometimes call it mesmerism. Dogs do likewise. An obvious case is the 'strong eye' in a sheepdog whereby sheep stand stationary, their gaze held by the dog, deprived of the initiative to move because the dog's will-power, transmitted through its eyes, is the stronger. The 'manning' of a falcon is achieved solely through the falconer out-staring the bird, his un-relenting will-power eventually dominating the resistance of the falcon which he confronts hour after hour until, without physical intervention, his determination prevails. Some people believe that pointers and setters can enforce immobility on partridges, pheasants and grouse through the eye in the manner of a sheepdog on sheep. I am not personally convinced of this, believing that it may be the sudden and sustained stillness of the previously fast moving dog which 'holds' birds to a point. But I am strongly convinced that the 'manning' of a gundog can be much assisted by the right use of human eye-power, and much retarded by its inadvertent misuse.

One late autumn day, a lady picker-up was less than totally happy with her labrador. We have all shared her feelings. She knew what the dog should be doing, she gave all the right signals, but response was lacking. She was not a bad handler. It was far from a bad dog, being neither riotous nor stupid, well trained by a capable professional. But they were not 'together'.

It being easier to solve a problem when one is not the handler concerned, I was ready with the answer when eventually she said, 'What the devil's the matter? He won't do a thing for me today.'

'Take your sun glasses off', I answered.

She did so, without comment, indeed tight-lipped. My advice had something near the devastating simplicity of 'Take up thy bed and walk'. She was experienced enough to know it. Confirmation was soon provided by the labrador. For the first time that morning he looked back for guidance when she sent him for a bird shot by her husband, and down in roots. The modern obsession with dark glasses amazes me. Earlier generations, my own included, have been able to withstand sunshine outdoors with the naked eye (including such modest glare as may be expected in England in November) and they have not been dazzled by electric light indoors. Yet younger people now wear dark glasses often enough to be unconscious of their presence – even in such particular circumstances as handling a gundog. Then, as the lady well knew, they cut the eye-contact on which the partnership depends.

Communication by eye has many applications in dealing with animals, but never more so than with dogs. All whose activities go beyond the pet stage know this. Equally, there are moments when the human eye is more than an animal can face, hence the elementary precaution of avoiding looking at a young dog bringing in a retrieve. The consequence of doing so is likely to be a hesitant, embarrassed approach, a hang-head, or a circling delivery.

In this situation something producing the effect of dark glasses can be a positive help, often an actual necessity, and most professional trainers make a habit of wearing a peaked cap. The head can then be tilted forward enough for the peak to hide the trainer's eyes as the dog comes in.

In more general exercises involving man–dog co-operation, the eyes are essential aids and must not become hindrances. The lady in question forgot that she was wearing dark glasses. How many of the rest of us remember that we are wearing glasses of any kind, or consider what the effects may be, and whether we are allowing for them? Having reached the time of life when I must always wear glasses, the subject has latterly been on my mind. I have realised that not only must I learn to live with glasses, but so must my dogs. For the reasons, consider again the basics.

Since dog-training involves the establishment of the trainer in the status of pack leader, a trainer must understand and employ the means which a canine pack leader would use to put thoughts into the minds of his subordinates. These go in not only through the ears, but also through the eyes, and it is as important to avoid conveying the wrong impressions as to transmit the right ones.

Throughout most of Nature, especially among carnivores, whether mammalian or avian, the sign of dominance, aggression and anger is the eye widely opened and focused on the other party. In brief, a glare. A tiger glares at the kill. A hawk's eye is a by-word. Fighting dogs enlarge their eyes, retracting the surrounding sinews and cuticle in doing so until the eye itself seems to bulge. Carvings in Indian temples of the more terrible gods in the Hindu pantheon reflect the influence over many centuries of people well placed to absorb the lessons of Nature, stressing in widened orbs the eye-power of Vishnu and Khali, omnipotent as creator and destroyer. This may seem a far cry from training dogs, but it is not. To use all his equipment a trainer must consciously perfect the histrionic trick of enlarging and rounding his eyes in moments of remonstrance, and narrowing them to slits in reconciliation or praise. This is what dogs themselves do. Fondle a dog, and note how its eyes almost close, only an elongated slit of the iris remaining visible. But a dog 'trying it on' with his handler enlarges his eyes as his ego swells relatively to that of his human partner. Dogs are as aware, if not more aware than we are, of human eye-expressions.

It follows that we must not give them a false impression of our own state of mind by failing to allow for the fact that we are wearing glasses. Still less must we risk cutting this important line of communication by completely hiding our eyes behind dark glasses. The latter, however, are not the only problems. The strongly defined horn frames of some clear glasses may in-advertently give to a dog an impression of the glaring eye of anger and domination, and undermine confidence in his handler, by appearing to enlarge the circumference of the eyes of the wearer. Human babies a few weeks old often burst into tears at the sight of such glasses, instinctively terrified at the face of the most benevolent of grandfathers if thus equipped. Perhaps rimless glasses, favoured by the late and unlamented Herr Himmler, may be helpful in dog training, or even in baby care. I do not propose to go to these lengths myself, but realising the possibility does no harm. It may even help, as a reminder of what may be overlooked.

Unquestionably sight is a less important sense than smell to a gundog. This variation in priority means that in any confrontation conducted in eye signs the trainer is, as it were, on home ground and may thereby have an advantage. The dog, dealing in his less favoured medium of communi-cation, may feel less self-assured. There are commonplace indications of this effect.

We act on the principle that seeing is believing. A dog does not. One's own dog will prove the point on any day's shooting. Momentarily out of contact in a crowded gateway, he will gaze anxiously first at one, then at another of the converging figures until he sights his master. But he will not immediately hurry forward, tail going, for the reassuring pat. He will approach with a try-anything-once diffidence to confirm by smell his visual impression. Only when his nose is satisfied are his troubles over. He does not believe his eyes.

Surprisingly, many shooters remain unaware of this. It is no rare experience to send a dog to retrieve a pheasant or hare lying in a furrow downwind on land newly ploughed, clearly visible but too far out for anybody to volunteer to walk out on the sticky going, and pick it up. The dog makes his initial cast, makes good the ground behind it by questing back across the wind, and casts himself again, still short of his target, and thus unable to wind it. 'Good heavens, can't he see it!' exclaims the Gun who cannot keep his mouth shut (there is generally one in every shooting party). His friends then have to decide between maintaining a charitable silence, and telling him the facts of life which include the dog's faith in its nose rather than its eyes.

It is more than probable that a dog would indeed have seen the game lying ahead of it. But the sight would mean nothing, the dog's awareness at such a time being geared strictly to its nose. To gundogs, with centuries of nose-consciousness bred into it, noses are for serious business, eyes merely come in useful occasionally. I have never needed to teach a dog to use its nose but, more often than not, have needed to inculcate the habit of using the eyes – notably, of course, to mark the fall of game. Nevertheless, it is remarkable how far away a dog can discern relevant small happenings which are not of immediate concern, while ignoring highly significant things close by, chiefly because they have not been indicated by scent, and are not moving.

An English springer spaniel over which I shoot has exceptional eyesight, which she uses no more than any other spaniel when doing her proper work, but from which she derives much interest when sitting at a stand. From a peg for driven partridges one October, facing eighty acres of plough sloping gently up to a skyline, she marked a hare traversing the beat ahead of the line a quarter of a mile out (almost invisible to me against the background of tillage, but possibly silhouetted at her elevation), and a single crossing partridge not much nearer. Without her indications I should have seen neither. It is worth mentioning in this context that she 'followed' each with her nose, pointing to the moving quarry and sniffing the air.

Perhaps it is because dogs feel less than total confidence in their eyesight that it is by eye that we most readily assert our will-power over them. A clear example, because it is a make-or-break point in the education of every gundog, is the 'sit-and-stay' exercise which generally comes early in the hand-training programme. Here the trainer can subject the puppy to the process of alternately exerting and relaxing the mental pressure through his eyes – a useful method, if not overdone, of demonstrating to a young dog which of the two is the supreme being. I do not like to make a dog feel 'small' unnecessarily, and never repeat this exercise after the point has once been made.

This consideration of the ways in which a dog can receive messages from its handler through its eyes prompts a treatment of the subject in reverse. A dog's eyes can tell its handler a great deal, some of it conclusive. Reference has already been made to the adverse impression made by a man who cannot or does not meet our eye; a gundog which does not do so is equally un-desirable. In any case he has put himself on the transfer list by that fact alone, provided I have had him long enough to be sure that he really is an evasive character, and not merely shy. Conversely, a dog that does meet one's eye, steadily and persistently of its own free will, can be forgiven a fair degree of original brainlessness. For such a one is honest and a trier. Give him time, and when he finds his purpose in the world he will have the unsurpassable virtue of reliability.

There is a difference, however, between the kind of message which a dog can take in through its eyes, and what it can give out. A dog can receive eye signals through the canine code to which he responds by reflex. But what a dog's eyes tell a man is more of an indication of general character than a declaration of immediate intent. For instance, whether the animal is biddable or defiant can generally be learned from its eyes, but not whether it is about to run-in, chase, or commit some comparable impulsive crime. It is possible for the human partner to declare after some such transgression that he saw 'a look in the eye' of his dog, and convince himself that he indeed did so. But those who interpret the 'look in the eye' with sufficient accuracy and promptitude to forestall indiscipline seem significantly few. In addition, it is seldom that a handler can see his dog's eyes in the situation when it decides to break. The only regular warning, and this in itself is a rare privilege, is the gathering of the muscles before take-off.

In assessing character through a dog's eyes one rule of thumb is repeat-edly confirmed. Rules of thumb, of course, are the encapsulation of other people's mass experience, and should not be taken lightly. I ignored this particular rule of thumb for years, and now regret having done so. It is the age-old preference for dark eyes. In times past I regarded this as just another semi-superstition and, thinking I knew better, dismissed it as such. Time has changed me from a tolerator of light eyes to a proponent of dark eyes.

To assert that all gundogs with dark eyes are superior to all with light eyes would be idiotic. The best spaniel I ever possessed had light eyes. But I have learned from trial and error, confirmed by the precepts of better men than I, that those seeking a trainable dog are more likely to find it among the dark-eyed than among the light-eyed. Dark-eyed dogs seem to possess an equability of temperament less often found in the light-eyed. They do not possess more brains, greater courage, better noses or more ready acceptance of discipline. They merely exercise more consistently such of these qualities as they possess, and hence are less prone to 'out of pattern' behaviour. I do not know any reason for this. Nor, to my knowledge, does anybody else. Presumably the equability gene and the dark-eye gene tend to associate together, as do the male gene and certain feather-pattern genes in sex-linked poultry. The circumstance is of value in reading a dog's character.

When the matter is carried farther, another question arises. How dark is a dark eye? Others may disagree with my opinion that although a dark eye is most desirable, it is possible for eyes to be too dark. Therefore my definition is that any eye is dark which is not indisputably a light eye. This permits a hazel eye, unless hard, to be regarded as dark.

Less this statement seems sibylline, it shall be analysed. We are concerned here with the eye, not merely as an organ for seeing, but as a conveyor of expressions. Some eyes are too dark for expression to be discernible, especially when set in the head of a black dog such as a labrador, a flat-coated retriever, a black cocker spaniel or a solid-faced springer. To 'read' such eyes at any range over ten yards under shooting conditions is virtually impossible. The face stares inscrutably back from the brambles or bracken, the eyes masked by the matching colour around them, as enigmatic as those of any poker player. A hazel eye, though less dark, may be more useful, subject to the foregoing qualification, simply because it is more visible.

My belief, again open to dispute, is that whereas 'hardness' can occur in eyes of all shades, it is more likely to be present, or at least noticed, in lighter eyes than in darker. There are blank, expressionless light eyes, commonly called 'goat eyes'. There are light eyes with the unblinking, non-informative character of car headlights. Some hazel eyes are eloquently soft. Equally, there are dark eyes as hard as ebony. Every day in recent seasons I have looked into a pair.

Sitting facing me at drives, a springer and a cocker have had their eyes on my face. They are about as dark-eyed as each other. There is no further resemblance.

The springer, despite a reputation for punching holes in cover, has eyes with a gentle fervour which seems to express, 'Thy will be done'. The cocker has eyes sparkling with a dominating vitality which emphatically declares, 'My will be done'. As keys to their natures, nothing could be more accurate.

Where no explanation for circumstances can be adduced, science is apt to deny the circumstance. Experience does not. However illogical the preference of experience-orientated gundog trainers for dark eyes, however subjective our deductions from the expression in those eyes, however mysterious the manner by which those expressions are produced, they provide means towards the trainers' ends.

5

HANDS AND HANDLING

Some people profess mild amusement that the term for the person who works a dog is 'handler'. The hands, they say, do not come into it. Perhaps it is indeed not a very good term to use. It was adopted a century or so ago when dogs were normally worked by kennelmen, grooms or gamekeepers, and no better one has turned up since. Everybody knows what it means, which seems sufficient justification now. But there is no justification for the mild amusement. The hands do come into it, though generally not nearly enough.

Touch is a neglected sense in the contact system between man and dog. Too often it is reduced to the mania for patting dogs which obsesses those who knew little about them, and the occasional, generally ineffective, slap for insubordination. When elevated above these levels, communication by touch can be given its own eloquence, and the effects which it then achieves are great.

Touch is another word for contact. All gundog training depends on contact; all its skills and disciplines are meaningless without it; maintaining contact is the central need and problem. Before contact can be maintained it must first be made. Before it can become an established understanding between man and dog it must begin as a physical act. It can hardly start too soon.

After their eyes open, but while still in the nest, puppies should become accustomed to being lifted, gently but firmly held, and gently returned to the bitch. The message must be that human hands are safe, and mean security. It is necessary that throughout the training process to come, and during its whole working life, a gundog should never be afraid of the man or woman in charge of it. Respect and fear are different. Fear undermines respect, and it is respect, not fear, which makes a sure partnership possible. From its earliest days a gundog-to-be must grow up with a strong faith in human nature, and a confidence in human beings as the solution and not the source of the problems it will encounter. Early handling, in and round the nest, is designed to build up this awareness of security in the human presence.

At six to eight weeks old, about the age at which many puppies go to new homes, the hands have a new role to play. Hitherto they have merely gentled; henceforth they will mould and direct. Not only are they now a key factor in the vital process of humanisation but they are beginning the educational process, though this is unknown to the puppy, which must remain in blissful ignorance for months yet.

It is easy to detect which puppies have been skilfully gentled in the nest and in the puppy run, and which have not. Those which already know the touch of Man come to hand, literally and figuratively, weeks quicker than those which have still to learn it. Early gentling was an *ad lib* operation but the stage has now been reached when the trainer's hands are actually starting chain reactions which will end in skills and style at work. So it is as well to begin with the basics of technique.

A puppy of three to five weeks, which at first can hardly crawl, then must learn to co-ordinate its legs, and even when an efficient mover has few clear ideas about where it wants to go, needs only to be made happy and safe. A month later its temperament and characteristics begin to be apparent. The trainer now has something to work upon.

If he is lucky he will have a puppy which is confident by nature without being pushed. At his approach such a puppy will sit looking up at him thoughtfully, unafraid but not willing to come forward and fraternise without further consideration, nor anxious yet to tear the toecaps off his boots. Probably the puppy is a thinker, perhaps with the sensitivity which is such a golden quality if properly used, and such a problem if not. The trainer will not be lucky with every puppy he takes on, but let us suppose for the moment that he is.

It is in the nature of humanity, until better ways are learned by analysing errors, to pat a puppy on the head somewhat in the manner of a bishop performing a confirmation. Respectable as the comparison may be, the habit of patting itself, and this application of it in particular, should be lost forthwith. More dogs than not dislike it. Though they will endure it, they regard it as a black mark against the perpetrator, and their respect for him is not enhanced. More useful contacts with a dog of any age are firm stroking, rubbing, and securer holding. There should be no roughness, but the animal should be given cause to deduce that strength underlies the caress. Nor should the element of play, with its consequences of excitability, form part.

The best place for rubbing is the chest, with a circular movement for enough time to make an impression, but not prolonged further. If this is combined with a downward stroking of the back with the other hand the effect on a puppy is soon apparent. Its attitude indicates gratification and trust; its eyes become narrow in contentment; and in all probability its head will be raised in that elevation essential in a creature which lives on ground level but is in the presence of its master – when, for instance, watching his face for orders, or delivering a retrieve. The habit of a raised head should be implanted early. It gives the same confidence to a puppy as smart saluting gives to a soldier. It is safer to implant it than to leave Nature to develop it. And the action of implanting it is the first man-made reinforcement of the alliance between trainer and trainee.

Thereafter throughout training, work and life as a whole, the touch of the hand will be meaningful to the dog, which will have come to expect it. In expressing praise, reassurance, caution, it can mean more than the spoken version of the same message, and is best conveyed that way, silence being golden in gundog work. The handwork should never be overdone, and always in response to a clear need or incident. That it happens at all should in itself be an event.

My own training method excludes the giving of titbits unless a desired effect can be achieved in no other way. Some English springer spaniels are so timid that the whole business of training daunts them, simply because it involves being given orders. For them I carry something edible in my pocket so that I can create in their minds the knowledge that this temporarily dreaded process contains at least some happy moments. In a few weeks young dogs previously so weighed down by their inferiority complexes as to be untrainable begin complaining vehemently when others are taken out and they are not.

This is different from associating a titbit with the performance of any specific task, which I believe should be avoided in all circumstances. It creates at least as many problems as it solves. A retriever, in my early days, was reluctant to relax her hold on her retrieves; though never hardmouthed in the sense of pinching her game, she held on to it with the tenacity of an alligator with lock-jaw. I tried the stratagem of holding, concealed, in my hand a piece of dried liver in such a manner that its scent would tell the bitch that it was there while I tried to persuade her to deliver. The result, as hind-sight indicates was inevitable, will surprise no old hand at the game. Thereafter the retrieve was spat out; the bitch could not wait to free her mouth for the reception of her reward. Basically, my misgivings against what are sometimes known as 'training baits' lie deeper. I do not believe in bribery.

I do not wish my dogs to serve me, however well, because they see me as a purveyor of delicacies. I wish them to do this because they think me worth serving for myself alone, and I am well aware that I must work hard to deserve their regard in such measure. It is the difference, in human terms, between being bought a drink or having one's hand shaken. If the man is big enough, gratitude is more acceptable the latter way. If dogs feel likewise, and I believe they do, the right touch from the guiding hand is worth much more than yet another routine nibble.

Hand contact has another all-important function. It maintains the image of infallibility and reliability if properly done. Animals do not like the hesitant half-hearted fondling which they so often get. Witness a horse stroked by somebody who, unfamiliar with the species, is not self-assured in approaching it. The light, tentative touch is probably ticklish and does no more than arouse suspicions and irritation signified by a restless shift of a foot, a petulant swing of the head, an ear laid back in boredom. A crisp clap on the muscles of the neck, firm enough to give off a healthy sound, has the opposite effect – cocked ears, eyes turned towards a visitor worth knowing the blown nostrils that indicate pleasure. So, with a dog, it is the touch of hands that proclaim themselves competent by their firmness, which makes a dog feel in better company. Gundogs are not saints. They exploit for their own advantage every laxity in those to whom they belong, seldom forgetting the ruses by which they can outsmart every individual human in their acquaintanceship. But the fact of their getting their own way does not elevate in their regard the person from whom they get it. Very much the contrary. Their loyalty goes to those who can command and hold it, and who in all their dealings with them give evidence of a sureness of hand. Touch, the right touch, is obviously a prime way of conveying it.

There will be times in every man–dog relationship in which all does not go smoothly. These, too, will involve touch. In all of them, we hope, the dog will come off second best. In doing so forcible arrest and restraint must sometimes be required. On occasions it will have something in common with a rugby tackle in spirit, even in execution, or in both. In other words, the comfort of the recipient cannot be guaranteed. In this case it is essential, subject only to the success of the enterprise, that the dog should emerge with the feeling of having brought his troubles on himself (i.e., he has been tripped over, sharply obstructed, uncomfortably grabbed). Whatever the feelings of the trainer, his levelness of bearing should not in such a case be compromised by revealing sympathy for the miscreant.

The occurrence of self-induced accident or discomfort is too good an opportunity to be allowed to go to waste. And it can be applied as a principle in some aspects of training. An example, especially useful because all factors in it can be kept under control, is in teaching a puppy how to walk on the lead.

The use of the lead will be more technically discussed later. We are now concerned with it purely as a device for the puppy's safety, for which it becomes necessary very early in a young dog's life. Almost certainly it will be the first physical restraint he has experienced. At first he will naturally disapprove, regarding the encumbrance round his neck as something accidental, like the bindweed in which summer-born puppies often become caught up when they try first their luck in an autumn hedgerow. He will shake himself to be rid of it. When this fails, he is likely to stand still, or to sit down, while he thinks out the problem. Unable to generate any worthwhile solution, he may then try to dash away.

All these reactions give the trainer opportunities of establishing himself in the puppy's mind as superior to surrounding circumstances, including such irritations as this. His policy should be to do nothing – absolutely and totally nothing, even in the smallest detail – except, perhaps, to speak reassuringly if the puppy shows signs of fear at its predicament.

He should not move. No attempt to walk on must be made until the puppy is ready to walk beside him without coercion. He should not attempt to tow the puppy by force, nor to cajole it by blandishments. When the puppy makes its getaway attempts (there will probably be several) he should stay silent and unimpressed. His hand on the lead must remain absolutely still, rigidly still. If the puppy's neck is to receive a painful jerk, the puppy's own action must cause it.

Faced with this impasse, the puppy's attention will slowly transfer from its misfortunes to the trainer himself. If it has been satisfactorily humanised, its mind will be receptive to the idea that he is the person who generally solves life's difficulties, so perhaps he can help in this one. The puppy will eventually move towards the man. When it does so, it should not be touched, because this would deflect its awareness of the lead. Instead, an encouraging sound should be made by the trainer, before he moves quietly on.

Perhaps the first move will be for only a few yards before the puppy again becomes puzzled and repeats its resistance. As has been said, dogs' memories are very short when young. If this happens the puppy should not be spoken to, rated, or told it is stupid. The same process is to be repeated – stillness until the puppy willingly accompanies, wordlessness except to allay fears, and the invariably rigid hand.

When the puppy begins to walk composedly beside the trainer, its undeveloped memory will ensure that its composure breaks down at frequent intervals, and that new escape tactics will be tried. The rigid hand must therefore be maintained to counter this. A sudden leap aside must provoke its own reaction in the form of sharp arrest, which is a significantly different thing from being pulled back, and while the hand must not yield, neither can it pull so long as it remains truly rigid. The realisation which percolates the puppy's mind is therefore one of immovable authority, immune to all attempts to shape it or gain a concession from it.

A non-rigid hand from which the puppy can jerk a mere six inches of liberty has in fact conceded. Admittedly the concession is only small, but no matter. Small beginnings open up large possibilities for both sides. On the human side authority is no longer immovable. On the puppy's side, momentarily it gained its point; and knows it. Henceforward, that gain may be exploited. The seed has been sown of that situation in which, mentally as well as physically, the dog comes to exercise the handler, towing him or her along, confident in its own mind that it is the dominant partner, hence prepared to defy control when the lead is removed; the reversal, in short, of the relationship which training is designed to create.

The value of the rigid hand is so great that two details can be added. First the length of lead between hand and puppy must be suitable. It must not be so short that the trainer's hand can be constantly felt; as when a horse is ridden on a short rein, this causes the puppy to fidget and fret. Nor must it be so long that the puppy comes to think that it has enough freedom in which to play around. Personally, I find it helpful to maintain the rigidity of my hand by carrying the lead in the usual manner across its palm, but tucking the thumb into my breeches pocket. This prevents the hand swinging, which is the negation of all control by the lead.

Consideration of this seemingly simple matter of early training on the lead raises a further point not directly concerned with the sense of touch, but with an application in every phase of the training process. It lies in the fact that the trainer has to wait for the puppy to generate of its own accord the willingness to accompany him. This may take some little time, even perhaps some long time, but it cannot be hurried without destroying the lesson which is being taught. Therefore, never train a dog against the clock; if there is a time factor, it is better not to train at all.

An acquaintance once said to me on this very matter, 'But I can't wait all day for the puppy to make up its mind!' Neither can I, often. But realities must be faced. It may be necessary to wait a long time, just possibly all day. Most people's lives do not offer unlimited opportunities for open-ended training sessions. Therefore those which do occur must be devoted to those exercises which may be time-dependent, and the habit be acquired of relating the training in mind not only to the ground available, but to the time available if needed. Most of us come to realise that the supposedly easy lesson (nothing could seem easier than teaching a puppy to walk on the lead, nor turn out in practice to be more difficult) can over-run its estimated duration by vast and inconvenient margins. This must be accepted, and its effects mitigated by due regard in advance for social, family and business commitments.

He who trains with his mind devilled by anxiety on some other matter will never generate the concentration necessary for success. The dog itself will be aware of his divided mind. Training must take place during hours when nothing else matters. To walk out on an autumn evening with a half-trained puppy to see sunset rabbits, and to return in black darkness to find one's family dined, and eager with a synopsis of the Ten O'clock News, is no rare experience. But the occasion must be carefully chosen.

As an extension of the same context, never train in bad weather. It is as great a misfortune to be forced to conclude a lesson, its point unmade, because heavy rain is making concentration difficult as it is to cut things short because the telephone may be ringing with an important and expected call. Time is not only the great healer; it is the great creator of understanding provided it is taken by the forelock in one of those fortunate interludes when, for some unidentifiable combination of reasons, a young dog is indisputably absorbing what it is required to learn.

Such situations are more probable in the later stages of training than in the earlier. Lead training has in itself nothing to do with gundog training. But it has much to do with that build-up of relationship in which the sense of touch plays so great a part. Wrongly accomplished, it can put the trainer–pupil bond under stress before it even starts.

Puppies three months old or less are not fit subjects for going on a lead, nor is there any reason why they should. In modern conditions the routine inoculations, without which no valuable dog should be off home ground, become effective at about fourteen weeks. By the time the puppy is four months old, real needs will occur for it to be under control on public thoroughfares, or in fields and woodlands. It is then, and not earlier, that the lead becomes essential. It should be made as nearly as possible an extension of the hand, irresistible and infallible.

6

By Nose and Tongue

The senses of smell and taste are closely related. We humans have used them less and less as our civilisation has developed, providing us with other means of picking up the messages which they once conveyed to our remote ancestors. To them smell was an information network reporting the invisible facts of their surroundings, its dangers and opportunities, what to hide from, what to pursue. Taste was a warning system telling what was poisonous and what was not. Now smell has become both a warning system and an appetiser, telling us what is undesirable and what is cooking. Taste with us has degenerated into a luxury whereby we relish our food and drink, making nutrition a pleasure as well as a necessity.

To dogs these two senses remain more nearly as they were to our remote ancestors. Smell is still the information network. Selective breeding has made gundogs even more skilful at interpreting it than evolution has made the undomesticated versions of their species, wolves and the wild dogs of Africa and Asia. Taste continues as a warning system and, so far as we know, as nothing else. Dogs seem greatly to enjoy the fact of having eaten but not, as we do, the act of eating.

With them the two senses, being relatively more important to them than they are to us, have not been blunted by increasing disuse. They are therefore greatly more efficient than the same senses are in humanity, giving them ranges of perception which we have long since lost. That they are so closely bound up with each other as to be almost interchangeable is readily apparent.

When a pointer or setter is on point, or drawing towards its point, it is catching the air, and the clues which the air contains, not only through its nostrils but through its mouth and over its tongue. The teeth are slightly parted, the tongue forward in the mouth; the flews flex inwards as the dog inhales great gulps of air orally, seeking to confirm its suspicion that game lies ahead. Foxhounds, 'brought to their noses' by the fading line on a bad-scenting day, behave similarly, their heavier flews flapping in and out as their mouths as well as their noses pick up the tainted air. They have not only been brought to their noses; they have been brought to their tongues as well; they are not only smelling fox but tasting fox with the atmosphere as medium.

These two senses, highly developed by evolution, not yet atrophied by civilisation but strengthened by selective breeding, are of great significance to all dogs, and to gundogs particularly. Through them gundogs become aware of most of what they want to know. How useful it would be if we could use these very influential channels to pass also what we want them to know into the minds of dogs. Unfortunately we cannot do this except in very limited and generalised ways, of which my grandfather's trick of putting a puppy's nose up his sleeve is an example. He knew that by this means the puppy would receive a more emphatic impression of his new master's identity than by any amount of looking at him, or listening to his voice – an undiluted dose of his personality, as it were. In the main, however, we cannot place messages for inward transmission through the noses and tongues of dogs.

But what we must not fail to do is to realise, and never forget even momentarily, that our dogs' noses and tongues are constantly picking up and passing on messages about us, whether we like it or not, whether we intend it or not. It is up to us to do what we can (which is admittedly little) to ensure that such messages serve our purpose if possible or, failing that, contradict them as little as possible. Let us consider nose messages first and not be prim about facing the undeniable fact that all of us smell.

What matters is what we smell of. Dogs have quite amazing powers not only of scent perception but also of scent analysis, which will be examined more fully later. Nevertheless I sometimes wonder how the air must seem to gundogs at, say, a covert shoot, especially after lunch. I myself, making no claims to unusual prowess in this direction, am generally aware of a wide range of aromas, most of them pleasant, but none the less distracting. Whisky, beer, port, Stilton and cigars are all readily identifiable by me. Perhaps I have a nose for these things. The dogs can no doubt distinguish between the stew, steak and kidney or game pie without which few well-conducted shoots are complete. If ladies are out, the range is correspondingly increased. Perfume, talcum and the rest are delectable in themselves and part of the varied patchwork which, via the dogs' noses, is their image of Man.

Those noses, of course, are immensely sophisticated and seldom deceived. For instance it has long surprised me that gundogs, which readily wind from forty yards away a decomposing pigeon shot a fortnight previously, are never confused by the overpowering reek of the stinkhorn fungus which spreads its smell of death in the autumn woods. Likewise hounds will take a line through sheep foil or a newly-opened silage pit, demonstrating the capacity of the canine nose to discriminate. One of our smells which we do not want the dogs we train to identify is the smell, normally imperceptible to us, which betrays nervous tension.

What remains to us of our own sense of smell is generally insufficient to detect this unless nervous tension is present in overwhelming quantity, for example in battle. Then it may become disturbingly manifest, as soldiers who have been in a tight corner well know. Evidently some adrenaline secretion through the perspiration system produces this effect which, once encountered, is never forgotten. My belief is that its occurrence is not limited to extreme stress, but is probably happening in some degree all the time when we are worried, mostly at levels too low to be apparent to the human nose but well perceptible to the more sensitive noses of animals.

If so, this may account for the familiar instances in which an animal which is jumpy and ill at ease with one human partner is coolly co-operative with another. One of them is in a state of anxiety, and so lacing the air with the chemical reaction to his own nervous tension; the other, being easy in his mind, is not. Cases are frequent in which a racehorse 'boils over' when ridden by an apprehensive work rider in training, but is calm and happy when ridden by a capable jockey in a race. One rider is scared, the other is confident, and the difference is revealed by the horse's behaviour. The parallel is the gundog which does not put a foot wrong out shooting but goes spare in a field trial. It is the same dog, the same handler, the same environment. The only difference is that the handler, who is untroubled by the demands of a day's shooting, knows that a field trial is competitive, becomes nervously tense, exudes adrenalin, and the chain reaction follows. Unfortunately there is no way by which we can stop ourselves exuding adrenalin, and horses and dogs becoming aware of it, except the near super-human one of controlling our thoughts.

The lesson for those of us with dogs in training is to reinforce the need for equability, of which much has already been said. A level head, a level voice yet with distinctive tonal contrasts, activity and competence, decisiveness allied to good humour are the requirements, whatever other inner feelings the trainer may have. If these equate to anxiety, conscious efforts must be made to quieten the mind and calm the nerves; if this is not done the uncontrollable emanations through the pores of our skin will give the game away. If we are nervous there is little hope of concealing the fact from a gundog of any age. The smell of unease and of fear is identical except in degree, and became too deep-rooted in the struggle for existence through which our ancestors passed to be disguised now.

Lion-tamers, horsemen, cattle men and gundog trainers must all sometimes put on an act, behaving as if we possess a confidence we do not feel. Knowing of the necessity, and the reason for it, it is possible to make a better job of striking such a pose than would be the case if the effort were made merely as a matter of form. It must be wholehearted enough to deceive ourselves if it is also to deceive our dogs.

If we do not transfer the direction of anxiety from worrying about whether the dog is under control to ensuring that we are under control, a shared apprehension will become atmospherically evident to the dog, and mutual confidence will be destroyed – not by some theoretical chain of neuro-pressures, but by a material reaction rooted in our mortal nature. There is no doubt that dogs, and probably all animals, are more susceptible than we are to this influence, and that, like so much else, it involves the sense of taste as well as that of smell.

In this connection we think too much of taste as a measure of pleasure or displeasure in nutritional intake. This distinction may not loom large to dogs. Throughout the animal range, food-discrimination is more often by aroma than by flavour. On the narrow question of palatability, texture is also of more consequence than flavour. On the more vital question of what is suitable to eat, smell tells a dog (or a horse or a cow) what is wholesome and what is not, what its system needs and what it does not.

Those glutinous descriptions of rich chunks of meat, long familiar in television advertisements, are designed to impress the dog-owners who have to pay for the stuff, not the dogs who have to eat it. Provided their food contains what they need, which is not everlasting meat, dogs eat it whatever it tastes like. The speed with which it goes down indicates that the attraction of savouring the supposedly luscious mouthfuls is not enough to make them linger over the pleasure. Healthy dogs swallow; they do not savour at leisure what they eat, nor pick and choose, nor chew. Dogs which have to be 'tempted' to eat have either been given too much already or are unhealthy in some other way.

That they have a more vital use for the sense of taste than mere enjoyment, and that this use may be linked to communication, is suggested by its use by dogs in contact-making. To us, of course, the contact with man is the most significant; especially the contact with 'master', equating with the leader of the pack, and our particular interest centres on the obsessional licking of the hand, and why dogs do it.

It may be argued, and indeed it has been argued by people with whom I have discussed the point, that this reflects a need for salt. We know salt to be present in perspiration which, however slight, is continuous enough to leave a salt deposit on the skin. It might also be argued, less plausibly, that certain nervous stresses create a need in the dog for instant salt and hence the urge to lick the hand, and there may be some force in the hypothesis too. But, if this were the total explanation, any hand would serve the purpose. But just any hand is not enough. The dog's desire is always for the 'master' hand.

Significantly, the desire to lick the 'master' hand is especially manifest after remonstrance. Some people assume (and in doing so attribute a human response to a non-human species) that an act of apology or subservience is being performed. I doubt both. Apology is a concept within the limits of the human mind, not of the canine mind. We confuse the issue if we credit dogs with our own thoughts. In inter-dog relationships, subservience is not indicated by tongue-contact. Instead, the subservient animal rolls or half rolls on to its back, exposing its throat (the attacker's main target) to indicate surrender. And the attacker, with rather more decency than humanity is apt to show in comparable circumstances, accepts the submission and peace ensues.

A dog will similarly half roll over at the feet of a man of whom it is for the time being in fear. But not until later, when the fear decreases or perhaps has passed, will the dog try to lick his hand, though the attempt will certainly be made before the incident is closed. Perhaps the word 'later' contains the key to the reason why. When provoked into nervous hyper-activity, as likely by anger as by the more normal stimulus of fear, adrenalin secretes through a man's pores. As the nervous reaction subsides, the taint of adrenalin also fades. So a reprimanded dog does not necessarily lick the master hand because it craves salt at that of all moments. The reason may be to check whether the adrenalin danger-sign is still present. In other words, to answer the crucial question, 'Does master still taste angry?'

If so, taste in the dog is established as one of the usual channels in the man–dog relationship, vastly transcending the minor part it plays in feeding to which our human thinking has reduced it. Since it may be possible inadvertently to transmit a message of anger to a dog via the touch of its tongue, or of fear via the evidence of its nose, it cannot be far-fetched to convey by the same means messages of attraction and confidence. Perhaps we do so all the time in some degree, without knowing it. What we must all do, all the time and in full consciousness, is to avoid sending the contrary messages by accident. This is the more feasible and more useful purpose to which we can put our knowledge of what the canine senses of smell and taste contribute to the canine mind.

As a practical example, taste, one's own physical taste generated in calm moments, can cement contact with one's dog. Formerly I applied a drill whereby, after I had reprimanded a dog, work or training was not resumed until the dog had touched the back of my hand with its tongue or nose (the senses being so conjoined, I combine them in this context as taste). My purpose was to make clear to the dog that the incident was ended, hence no longer an obstacle to mutual confidence. The effect surprised me. The link between us was obviously so strengthened that to use the taste-touch only after reprimand seemed to be both under-valuing it and under-employing it. In the first place, it became associated inevitably with the aftermath of strained relations. Secondly, it could then be used only in circumstances which one hoped would not occur often.

When one holds a trump card one looks for the chance to play it. I found an extended use in the teaching of spaniels to hunt in a pattern. Fundamental to this is close crossing in front of the handler by the questing dog. By clicking my tongue and holding out my hand at every fourth or fifth pass, I enabled the dog to make a touch without breaking its stride. This reduced the tendency to pull ahead, and gave the pattern that shape of a flattened elipse which is the ideal foundation for all but downwind work. As soon as this was established, I discontinued the touch drill. There was no marked deterioriation. By that time the pattern was second nature, with or without game scent. More important, I am convinced that dogs which have been trained in this manner have been more 'with me' than dogs which were not. Whether this is so or not is to some extent beside the point. The fact that I think it is, and am in consequence more confident and relaxed, constitutes a decided gain.

II
WITHIN THE DOG

7

THE CANINE MIND

Having assessed the points of entry into a dog's mind, and some of the messages which might be conveyed through them, the question arises of what use the canine brain can make of the information received. In considering its responses our conclusions can be deductive only, an analysis of general experience, which is one of the reasons why gundog training is an art, not a science. None of our beliefs are capable of specific proof by measurement or in other terms which would be scientifically acceptable. Those which are offered here are put forward in the knowledge that they will be critically examined by many persons with good reason to trust their own judgement, and if I err it is on the side of caution.

Since the mental capacity of a dog roughly equates to that of a bright three-year-old child, it is subject to the same limitations. Observe a bright three-year-old child first at solitary play, then in the company of others of its age-group, finally with older persons. It is evident that such a child can do one thing at a time, but if asked to do simultaneously two things which singly it can do efficiently and with satisfaction is unable to comply. To build a wall with toy bricks is within its compass and a pleasure; to listen to a story is another pleasure. But if told a story while playing with bricks the child will either drop or ignore the bricks or fail to comprehend the story. A year later he will build even better toy brick walls, and absorb the story simultaneously, because a child's brain continues to develop beyond the human age of three. The brains of very few dogs do so.

Within this limitation of non-development and one thing at a time, the brains of working bred gundogs operate vigorously, reliably and willingly. But no matter how gifted with what we loosely (and often erroneously) describe as 'intelligence', dogs cannot exceed their destined capabilities, the mechanism to do so not being present. We therefore have a potentially efficient source of responses and initiatives, powered by a very considerable ancestral heritage of aptitudes and ambitions. We have five lines of communications with it, one for each of the senses. Three of these are of major significance – sound, sight and touch; two are relatively minor as communication media man to dog – smell and taste.

Dogs bred for 'biddability' (readiness to comply with human wishes) have great sensitivity to messages passed through any of the first three senses. But here the first limitation operates. Though messages by all the five senses can motivate a dog's brain, that brain can deal with only one form of input at a time. If messages are conveyed to a dog through two of its senses, one will cancel the other unless sufficient interval is left between them. Otherwise the mental switchboard will be jammed, so to speak. Examples are repeatedly encountered.

A retriever which has learned to walk heel-free pulls on a stride ahead. Its handler can do one of two things. He can growl at it, or he can slap it on the quarter with the lead. In either case the dog will be reminded that it is out of its ground, and will drop back into its proper station. But if the handler does both, neither message is certain to be acted upon, still less remembered. The slap on the quarter, in itself enough to restore good order and discipline, will be cancelled out by the handler's voice, since most dogs will go to any lengths to be spoken to, and regard even a hostile word as forgiveness; or the handler's voice and the dog's consequent intention to comply will have coincided with a slap on the quarter. In the first instance the desired impression will have been instantly removed, in the second it will have been distorted into confusion. Hence the value of a wordless correction. Not only is it more effective, it is safer.

Another familiar situation is that in which a retriever, sent for an unmarked bird, is short of its target area. The handler blows his whistle to attract the dog's attention, gives the accepted signal to the dog to extend the range, and calls 'Go back' or 'Get out', according to his choice. These are all very proper things to do in such a situation, but are governed by the overriding stipulation, 'It's not what you do, it's the way that you do it.' Here the differences creep in, and are decisive. Before commenting further it should be added that all the indiscretions mentioned in this book have been freely committed by me in full view of the public, and doubtless will be again. In that way I have learned how disastrous their effects can be.

Contrast the techniques of an enthusiastic amateur and a seasoned professional in the case in question. Both obtain the dog's attention. But the amateur, heartened by this response, is over-quick to exploit it. His hand signals and voice command come concurrently. The dog then has messages coming in by ear and eye simultaneously. He makes what he can of a signal system which has now lost its clarity and absorbs only the general drift, eventually getting on with the job in his own way – and learning, incidentally, that life is simpler if human wishes are disregarded. The professional is in so such hurry; he knows he will save time by using a little more of it. To him obtaining the dog's attention is nothing remarkable, but it is an asset he is determined not to squander. He therefore does nothing immediately but waits, with the dog's eyes on his face, while its anticipation builds up, keeping it waiting and thereby increasing its eagerness for the next order. A keen dog in such a situation bunches its muscles in readiness, as a horse is collected for maximum effort when presented at a jump. Then, without haste but with painstaking deliberation, the handler pushes out his hand in one single action, sending the dog towards the game. He does not, at that stage, speak. If the dog shows signs of again hunting short of the target area he has the minatory 'Go back' available to keep him going, whereas the amateur had expended its first impact and could use this command only in repetition, inevitably with diminishing effect.

The professional had kept his commands sufficiently separate for the dog to assimilate them by ear, eye, ear successively but without confusion. Even a child aged three could have understood him.

The inference for us is that we do not increase the output of the canine mind by stepping up the input. More commands do not mean more action. The reverse is the case, because if orders are given more rapidly than they can be dealt with, the dog's concentration on those already given is broken. Unnecessary, even meaningless orders like calling 'Hi lost' to a dog which is already hunting purposefully, cause breaks in concentration. The point is important because the prime essential in employing the canine mind in the service of Man is to get it to concentrate on what Man wants it to do – the gundog on game, the sheepdog on sheep, the guard dog on burglars – at first in a general way and eventually in terms of the specific task of the moment.

To leave the maximum amount of clarity in the minds of dogs at work, the minimum necessary amount of commands and signals should be put into them. Remember King Lear, they should never be bethumped with words. This is why the best handlers button their lips, leave their whistles hanging, put their hands in their pockets, and in all ways keep a low profile whenever there is no pressing need for a further command – as when an experienced dog is working satisfactorily in the area desired.

Young dogs uncertain of their tasks sometimes need vocal encouragement pending development of their full confidence. Here reiteration of the most over-reiterated of all gundog expressions, 'Hi lost', has its passing value. But some people use it as if it were a magic formula and only its constant repetition half-a-dozen times a minute will keep a dog working. There are certainly some dogs which stop working unless constantly reminded to carry on, but the remedy in these cases is not to make the welkin ring. Such dogs should be retired and better ones bought. Their presence, and the vociferation they necessitate, upsets other and better dogs which are capable of working well in silence.

Having written hard things about the shooting man's tribal cry, it remains to say that there are three useful applications of 'Hi lost' in addition to a greater number of misapplications. It is useful to indicate:

(a) that game is down and needs finding;
(b) to tell a young and doubtful dog which is beginning to despair on an as yet unproductive hunt, 'All right, you're doing fine.'
(c) to tell a dog, sent for a bird it was not able to mark, when it has reached the area to be hunted.

Its chief misapplication is its use as a call sign by a handler who has lost his dog, and does not wish to admit it.

Given simplicity and clarity, gundogs of any category have enough mental equipment for all and any of the tasks normally given to them, subject to two reservations. The first concerns the heady element of inherited desires and aptitudes, more fully covered in the next chapter. Their relevance here is that they involve the vitalising element of live game scent. This, the fuel of the gundog libido, releases awareness and energies which lie dormant in its absence. Only reactions, or lack of them, noted in the presence of live game scent should be considered in estimating the worth of a dog, or assessing its training needs. Live game scent has the effect of putting the canine brain into over-drive. Pressures build up which are imperceptible in other circumstances, communication systems break down – dismissed by the dog as beneath its notice in face of this new and overpowering attraction. Unless the man–dog link has been properly conceived and forged firm enough in earlier training, the cumulative internal stresses awakened by live game scent will produce the kind of disappointments which bring the owning of gundogs close to being a heart-break. An obvious example of this is whining.

To gundog owners 'whine' is the most depressing word of all. It has probably ended more high hopes than any other. The dog that whines on shooting days has more than just a fault. First, whining is generally incurable so the noises-off must be accepted for the dog's lifetime (and inflicted on other people), or the dog must go. Secondly, most people hold it to be hereditary, so breeding from a whiner is out; nobody would wish to keep a puppy, and nobody 'in the know' would buy one. Thirdly, and unkindest cut of all, the dogs that whine generally possess willingness, courage and initiative in high degree; many of us have had cause to say, 'It's always the good ones that do it.'

In my opinion, nothing can be done to cure it if the habit has become established. There are recommended cures and amelioratives. Some are picturesque enough to indicate the desperation in which they originated. The late Leonard Crawley, the Test Match cricketer and amateur golf champion and talented dog handler, devised a blindfold for his labrador bitch to wear during drives. To me it was as much a rogue's badge as blinkers on a race-horse. Though initially successful it also seemed likely that whereas she had previously whined at the sight of falling birds, she would in due course whine at being blindfolded. I never had the heart to ask him if this proved so; nor did I hear the glad news that the trouble was cured.

Some say that a squirt of harmless liquid from a siphon or aerosol admin-istered at first squeak stops the noise. That is for others to try; not for me, being a shy man anxious to avoid notoriety. However, I have seen a lady standing with her husband and retriever in line, popping cartridges with one hand and holding a soda-water siphon in the firing position with the other. The marriage survived, but they divorced the dog. There is also the tra-ditional advice that taps on the dog's head with a twig, timed to interrupt its thoughts of whatever makes it whine, can effect a cure. Again, not for me. I lack the X-ray eyes to read a dog's thoughts through its skull, and in any case have no wish to behave like a jazz drummer when there are other things to do.

It seems more sensible to regard *every* dog as a potential whiner, and therefore to take all practical steps to prevent the trouble arising, even when there are no grounds to suspect it. I do not believe the whining *per se* is in-herited. But I do believe that the characteristics which make whining likely are inherited, a distinction which is by no means without difference. Since these are mostly desirable, if they can be separated from whining, the need is for prevention rather than cure. This must take the form of eliminating the cause of the whining.

We deceive ourselves if we regard the whine as a fault in itself. It is a symptom of something, and cannot be eradicated without detriment to future generations simply by 'breeding it out'. Gundogs bred to be so unenthusi-astic that they found nothing to whine about would be of little use. The cause of whining may not be wholly, or even primarily, in the dog. It may origi-nate in the trainer, or in the eventual owner. It could result from an excess of repression over leadership by the man or woman in charge. Put differ-ently, the dog is asked to bottle up the inherent drives which are released by live game scent – those to hunt, to retrieve, and so to please its master – but is not given any alternative expectation. This repression therefore takes the purely negative form of 'Whatever you want to do, don't do it' without substituting the compensation of 'Here we are together; let's enjoy ourselves; keep an eye on me for the signal'. Faced with the former drab prospect, rather than the more attractive second prospect, the dog whines in disappointment.

A whiner can be produced in no time at all (and years ago I did so) simply by taking shooting a dog with all the right instincts, but which does not yet regard its master as its pack leader. To avoid the frustration which causes whining it must have had time and good reason to accept its master not merely a brake on its ambitions but also as the architect of its pleasures and the source of the best of its fun. Disaster is accelerated if the dog is taken shooting too young for this dual role to have become apparent.

So with the humility which comes of having made the mistake three times, which is twice too often, my conclusion is that a whiner is almost certainly a potentially good dog which was allowed to learn the meaning of game scent and the power of the gun before its master had made himself important enough in the dog's eyes. The man, not the dog, initiated the fault. The man can still restore the situation in the limited number of the cases in which action is taken soon enough. The problem may well be complicated by the possibility that a whining dog does not necessarily know that it is whining, or may be whining virtually all the time, but unheard by us because doing so at frequencies too high for human ears to hear. A dog can hardly be expected to realise that a falsetto whine is tolerated but a soprano whine is a crime. Nevertheless that is what I think we may be asking dogs to do. Research will one day clarify the point.

Whatever the inner details, whine is a product of the extra pressures imposed when live game scent and the presence of the gun raises the tempo (though not, of course, the scope) of the canine mind from normal into overdrive. All the disciplines, relationships and securities which training has inculcated at the normal level must be strong enough to survive this transition without breaking down. When its tempo is fully activated by live-game scent a dog's mind works not only extremely rapidly but much more more rapidly than its trainer, of all people, is likely to appreciate, he having become accustomed to its lower-level speed of thought. Chance gave me the opportunity of seeing the effect of this in the matter of a retriever's acceptance of direction by hand signal.

Somebody had filmed a field trial, in the course of which a lady handler met misfortune because when signalled to go left her alert and seemingly co-operative golden retriever, sent for a bird it had not seen shot, had three times gone right. In consequence it perpetrated a 'first dog failure' and was eliminated. At the time all that her rivals could do was to commiserate. Later, when we saw the film, we knew the reason.

The handler in question is an athletic young woman, and right-handed. She gave, as is normal, all her signals with her right hand and arm. But the camera recorded what the eye did not, and this was that in giving her executive signal to the dog to go left – an extra-vehement punch across to the left – she first moved her arm a few inches to the right, instinctively to give the gesture extra force, in the manner of a golfer addressing the ball. The film not only showed this very clearly, but it did not fail to record the eyes of the dog and its other reactions. The eyes clearly followed the short rightward travel of the hand, and the dog was moving in that direction before the gesture she really intended was made. Not for nothing do professionals give this form of direction indication with extreme deliberation and very slowly. They have learned the hard way the unconscious idiosyncracies of handling styles, the hair-trigger reactions of keen, fit gundogs and the truth that, as sure as guns recoil, every gundog virtue has its compensating fault to be guarded against.

The limitations in the scope of the canine mind do not correspondingly restrict its depth. Instinct has left several built-in skills, inherited from the struggle for existence in the dog's evolutionary history. Awareness of location is one, in a sense separate from the eye for country to which reference has already been made. This awareness becomes operative even when dogs are in an environment which insulates them from knowledge of their surroundings; for example, in a dog box fitted inside the car.

Our travelling box has a ventilation grille facing forward, and visible from the driving seat through the internal rearward mirror. This enables me to keep a degree of observation on the dogs' welfare during journeys home from shooting, normally between ten and twenty-five miles, but occasionally a hundred or more. After a day's work they sleep through the return journey, but invariably wake when we are between one and two miles from home.

For long I presumed that even in sleep their senses were attuned to sequences of speeds, gradients and turns which, in certain combinations, forewarned the approach of journey's end. Then an episode indicated the possibility of something more. There are three roads into our village. Two of them turn sharply off a main road two miles away. A lively pace along the main road, deceleration, change of direction, and then the leisured progress through the lanes would make a recognisable pattern. If this were perceptible in sleep the fact would be remarkable enough but understandable, especially as these are the roads by which we normally approach the village. The third road links with no main road, but is merely a tentacle off a twenty-mile network of lanes, the gradients of which are wholly different from those of the other approaches. It is also an approach which we very seldom use and never, so far as I could recall, on return from shooting. Yet when, after a detour to visit a friend fifteen miles out, I did complete a journey that way my dogs in the box woke up, stretched, and thumped their tails when we were a mile-and-a-half from home.

So much for the mental norm of gundogs in general. Superimposed upon it are the exceptions, the super-bright and the infra-stupid. Here the variations are quite wide, and it is difficult to separate exceptional natural talent, fortuitously bequeathed on individuals by inheritance, from the exercise of exceptional gumption by individuals gifted with better-than-average brains, or with an environment in which brains can develop. Natural talents include a good nose, eyesight, pace, agility and stamina. Gumption of course means the effective use of these and all other faculties.

Vincent Routledge, a great man of gundogs in general and retrievers in particular, once said that the quality he most valued was brains – more, even, than a good nose. Anyway he had found that dogs with brains generally had good noses also. Put another way, it may be that in degree of acuteness in the physical senses, of which 'nose' is one, few dogs are markedly better or worse than others, but some have better brains than others and so make better use of the information which their senses bring them. A bright dog, hitting a touch of scent, is prompt and thorough in exploiting every possibility surrounding it, and on getting another touch recognises a pattern beginning to form, ending by a find which is generally attributed to a good nose. But his nose, in isolation, may be no better than that of a duller dog which also hit the touch of scent, but lacked the intelligence to exploit it to the point of success.

The paramountcy of the brain, in activating to best advantage the physical senses used in gundog work, is not dependent only on its acuteness. Its stamina is equally important. We see the canine brain tire *before* the canine body does, and this disguises the fact that it tires *because* the canine body does, some unaccountable minor lapse often being the first symptom of organic fatigue not yet made apparent by a flagging of the dog's action. This is the reason for the great importance of fitness in all gundog work, especially of course in competition. The material consequence of lack of it is not that the dog lies panting from its exertions (though it may well do so), but that it becomes inefficient at those critical moments which, because they demand the quickest and most accurate reactions from the dog, are also crucial for the shooter. Where the reaction is neither quick nor accurate nobody needs much reminding of the forms which failure and frustration may take.

A bird dog runs into a covey, flushing them out of shot and denying the Guns the opportunity he is employed to provide. The strain was telling on his ill-prepared physique. Though he was galloping as hard as ever, his nervous system's telegraph, which should have ordered him to stop and freeze on point at the first touch of scent, did not operate fast enough. Or a retriever, still the epitome of willingness and effort, misses a bird he would normally have found; no longer thorough enough, he missed the yard of ground where it lay. Or a spaniel, winding rabbit, turns to the scent that little bit too slowly, allowing the rabbit to reach its bury instead of being flushed into open ground. Small though the initial causes may be, all result in game remaining on the wing or on foot instead of being in the bag; and to put game in the bag is the fundamental purpose of all gundogs.

The canine brain has other characteristics better learned in advance than discovered by experience. One is that in certain circumstances it is drained of energy and placed under stress by the effort of decision-making. The circumstances are those in which the decision is not reflex but the result of deliberation. A retriever confronted by two pheasants, both active but one wounded and the other not, would decide to catch the first and ignore the second by reflex activated by the scent of blood on the bird which had been hit by a pellet. The action occupies only a split second; the dog is probably unaware that decision was necessary. It is different when a dog has to decide which is the least of two or more evils. Instead of the decision being dictated to him, he himself must make it.

A spaniel has retrieved a duck from the far side of a river, and the arrival platform is a steeply sloping, slippering bank. On the outward journey he was unaware of it, since he entered the water with a leap, so was airborne when he crossed. On the way back, now waterborne and laden with the weight of the duck, the prospect is daunting. From the line of high ground ahead, looking cliff-like to him swimming below it, he must choose the least difficult point at which to climb out. Observe what happens.

He swims up and down the bank, encouraged by his handler who is rightly letting him know he is not alone. Eventually he makes up his mind, and with whatever effort is required climbs out and delivers his burden, doubtless to the praise of the human spectators. But as he pants and shakes himself, temporarily drained by his labours, he does so not only from the weariness caused by swimming, which is likely to be the least of his problems, but from the depletion of nervous energy and the aftermath of stress resulting from the problem he had to solve. It is to be hoped that in that triumphant moment nobody examines the bird carefully. Had this happened, its ribs might have been found to be stove in.

Twice the following sequence of events has happened in my sight, in each case the bird retrieved being a running hen pheasant, more easily damaged than a duck. On each return voyage the pheasant was couched in the dog's mouth, its head up, in that curiously contented and relaxed attitude of game birds which are firmly but comfortably held by a dog with a good mouth. During the swimming up and down the bank while the dog chose the least forbidding landing place this attitude was maintained until the dog turned at right angles to the bank preparatory to climbing out. It was at that stage, before the climbing process began, that each pheasant's head dropped. The prospect of the climb, or tension attendant on the dogs' marshalling of their forces for the effort, had caused the grip on the birds to be tightened to a lethal pressure. The effort of the climb itself did not.

For similar reasons a vulnerable moment for game being carried, alive or dead, comes when the returning dog is confronted by high forestry wire and runs along it seeking a place at which to jump. Very probably the dog 'flew' the wire without hesitation on the outward journey, but coming back is a different story. There is then something to carry, and the only manner in which a dog can do so is disadvantageous. The load, being held in its jaws well ahead of the centre of gravity, corresponds to a loaded tray carried by a waiter at the full extent of his arms. This not only increases the apparent weight but causes maximum disturbance to the balance of a dog which has to climb a steep slope or jump an obstacle. The effect must be a depletion of the reserves of physical energy, but this depletion is evidently of less effect than the run-down of nervous energy in all cases where the dog must make a decision involving the resolution of a doubt. Doubt in any form is very difficult for the canine mind to cope with. Hence the needs for clarity and confidence in all relations between man and dog.

The counter-measure to doubt is concentration. The dog must be given something constant, unassociated with any doubt, on which to concentrate. In practice this can only be the handler himself. He must make himself a factor of greater weight in the dog's consciousness than the many impon-derables which it will have to meet. The man, in short, must by the mere fact of his presence constitute a sort of splint to strengthen the potentially wandering concentration and vulnerable confidence of the dog. He must mean much to his dog, and his dog must mean much to him, not merely when they are out shooting but always, for another peculiarity of the canine mind is that a dog is very readily aware when it is being ignored.

It is not possible to switch off a dog, converting it from a living, conscious creature with an adoration complex for the man in its life, into something akin to a piece of apparatus which is not required until further notice. The man–dog link is a continuous thing. There is no need to be demonstrative about it, but there is a very real need to behave in such a manner as to keep it alive. Here, I think, the kennelled dog has one of its advantages over the house-kept dog. A dog in a kennel cannot be 'cut dead'. But a busy master, in hurrying to answer the telephone, may cause deep and unintended offence to a dog he walks past without noticing.

Establishing the handler (whether or not he is the original trainer) as the supreme being in the dog's life is the foundation on which all gundog training eventually rests. It is possible, sad to say, to train a dog in all the skills and drills he needs to know without the trainer attaining this status. A dog trained by somebody whom it does not come to respect may know its job and its disciplines as well as any other, but it will not necessarily carry them out in the heat of action and the height of temptation.

A personal anecdote illuminates the point. A spaniel of impeccable field trial breeding had all the necessary attributes. She was quick, clever, stylish, brave and full of game sense. Not surprisingly, I held her in high esteem, and made the elementary error of assuming that her regard for me was commensurate with my regard for her. It was not, as events proved. Consequently she disobeyed whenever this course suited her, and in effect defied me to prevent her continuing to do so. I did not take up the challenge because a friend bought her – well knowing, I may say, of her failings, having been forewarned that her niche in life would probably be as a duck shooting dog (quick action, self-determination, and no questions asked).

Soon afterwards I discovered that my reputation as a trainer had gone up several notches. The bitch was being hailed as the ideal spaniel. Her new owner generously disclaimed all credit, on the ground that I had trained her, and he had taught her nothing. She was mated to a Field Trial Champion, her litter was over-subscribed in advance by shooting men who had admired her work, and a wide circle basked in her reflected glory. Many people were happy: some because they had acquired puppies, her new owner because he said he had the dog of a lifetime, and I because I had got rid of her. All that had happened was that he had made himself her supreme being, which I had not.

In this connection some facts have recently become available of special interest to those who breed or buy-in a young puppy for training. They concern the stages of development of the canine mind in early youth, long before the age at which training can begin, and their effect on the relationship with human partners. They have emerged from the carefully recorded and monitored observations of many purpose-bred puppies and thus have a special validity in this context, although the puppies in question were not destined to be shot over.

Understanding animals is a matter of experience. We all know this, without invariably realising what it means. The experience must be with the animals themselves, in health, in normal environments, doing what they are intended to do, be it only to put on weight. Those who see most animals at first hand over the greatest number of years are able to keep their eye in, to lose their illusions, sub-consciously to analyse temperaments, and in general to know their stuff. This excludes vets *per se*, who see many sick animals but have no reason to see more fit ones than other people; and commentators such as myself, my life so far having brought me into first-hand knowledge of fewer than a hundred each of dogs and horses. Those whose opinions are worth heeding can count their similar contact-knowledge in thousands – dealers, farmers, some race-horse trainers, huntsmen, farriers in cavalry regiments (what few remain) and, of present significance, the staff of the Guide Dogs for the Blind Association.

This organisation has been based on the pooled knowledge of people reflecting many different interests in dogs, and possessing many varied skills. From my contacts with its trainers I know that they include a competitor in sheepdog trials, a successful whippet racer, and several gundog enthusiasts; and gundog breeds provide the great majority of guide dogs, because of their intelligence and tractability. Get enough dogs, and enough intelligent people, constantly observing, recording and quantifying, and useful facts emerge. The Guide Dog service is to produce a constant succession of dogs sufficiently well trained and reliable to be entrusted with human lives in face of modern life's greatest danger, the traffic. The dogs are bred on progeny test criteria because guide dogs themselves are unsexed before they become capable of breeding. Breeding stock and working stock are closely observed from whelping to retirement and this process has produced many conclusions, one being of special interest to owners of sporting dogs.

Mr Derek Freeman, head of the Association's breeding and puppy-walking service and an all-round dog man with detailed knowledge of the retrieving breeds and a private interest in training German Shepherd Dogs (Alsatians), has pin-pointed the vital influence on a dog's entire life of what happens between the ages of six and nine weeks. His findings have been confirmed by monitoring the subsequent histories of four thousand puppies. Mr Freeman places the first three weeks of a puppy's life as beyond human influence, except in ensuring it security, warmth, cleanliness and nourishment. In the following three weeks puppies need continued security. Guide

Dog puppies all receive human handling to teach them sensitivity to touch, and chances to recognise the approving human voice, the aim being to predispose the puppy towards accepting orientation towards humanity when the time for it arrives.

Then come the most vital three weeks in the life of dogs which are required to co-operate closely with a human partner – the joint destiny of guide dogs and gundogs. Left to themselves, puppies become progressively less conscious of their dam, and progressively more conscious of each other from three weeks onwards. From the sixth week onward the growing awareness of each other hardens into a realisation of their place in the canine community, the rest of the litter representing for the time being the whole race of dogs. If removed from the company of its siblings before the hardening of its integration into the community of dogs, a puppy will transfer the relationship to whatever human being replaces them. Thereafter, its reference to the desires and habits of the pack of puppies being no longer possible, it will find security by conforming instead to the wishes and customs of its masters. Instead of a canine pattern being imprinted on its developing psyche, a human version is implanted. But not so clearly, or so easily, if the puppy is eight weeks or more.

Separation earlier than six weeks causes too many problems and stresses to be worth doing. Mr Freeman quotes work by Scott and Fuller as indicating that from seven weeks on the capacity to make the human transplantation recedes. The inference is that eight weeks, the conventional age for taking over a puppy, is at least a week too late where the puppy is intended for a working role in co-operation with a human partner, including of course the role of a gundog, and that the optimum age for take-over is six weeks and three days. Puppies put out to walk at or about this age take, on average, two months less to train as guide dogs when, more than a year later, they return to the Association's kennels.

Most of the dogs which I have trained have been home-bred. Four, however, were bought. I checked their case histories through our kennel records, in which dates are recorded with precision, and comments are added as training and work progresses – though without the thoroughness of the Guide Dogs system. A five-year-old cocker bitch, who needed a whole season to learn that she was not merely working, but working for me, had been taken over at nine weeks and three days. An English springer, to whom I did not have to tell anything twice and whose eyes were always on mine, had arrived at six weeks and six days. A cocker aged twenty-two months, whose every movement flows towards me and who is one of life's great triers, was collected at seven weeks and one day (in order to be sure of pick of litter).

An English springer aged one year was generously kept by her breeder until twelve weeks; I later wished he had not been so kind.

After infancy, a dog's life becomes more complicated, more subject to variables arising from the facts that as individuality develops no two dogs are identical and neither are any two men and women. Definition of the staging points in a dog's march to maturity therefore becomes less precise. There are, however, some observable signs which I have found useful in assessing the progress and prospects of young dogs in training.

First, the attainment of a full mouth makes a puppy less preoccupied with sensations in its gums and thereby removes an interruption to concentration in its lessons at retrieving. These in themselves have a significance transcending the mere act of retrieval. Because they involve the puppy in rendering a service, retrieving lessons are invaluable in establishing in the puppy's mind the relative positions of the two members of the partnership. They demonstrate that the two-legged one is more than just a large and cheerful playmate, or the nice chap who brings in the food, but that he represents authority and has the capacity to exercise it.

Secondly the fixation of memory at or soon after eight months is roughly co-incidental with a significant physical indication. It is then that the skull broadens. Actually, as well as in figure of speech, there is suddenly more between the ears. Previously the puppy's narrower head and accompanying air of intermittent daftness equated with the immaturity and fits of irresponsibility of human adolescents at the discotheque stage. Now it is replaced by an appearance of maturity which is generally reflected in the animal's attitude to life. To me this change, so strikingly swift and unheralded, gives great encouragement. Most of the frustrations which crop up in the weeks preceding it, the lapses of memory and uncharacteristic thick-headedness, can be dismissed with the thought that such things will not happen when the skull has broadened. Comfortable words, perhaps, but unlike most such, events have nearly always proved them true.

Thirdly, and not surprisingly, the completion of first heat gives a bitch a placidity generally lacking before it. These are all instances which mark the time-scale in which training proceeds. Time is the element which cannot be stimulated, hastened, delayed or ignored; but which must always be given. And the only time-element which has validity is that which is calculated from the date of the dog's birth, not from the commencement of training. The latter is irrelevant, especially if too soon.

Distinction must be drawn between the canine brain and the canine mind. The brain is material and finite, the organ of tissue, blood and other fluids which occupies the skull. The mind is what happens, apparently inside it, under the influence of genetic inheritance, human control and experience. Some characteristics of the canine mind are subjective in the sense that though we may have reason to believe they exist, they cannot be proved.

Two have already been mentioned – the possibility of extra-sensory communication between man and dog, and the dog's unexplained sense of orientation and location in which an extra-sensory element also seems sometimes present. Two others suggest that the canine mind also has a moral plane, either inherent or implanted.

That dog does not eat dog is an ancient truism. But neither does dog kill dog with anything approaching the frequency with which man kills man. Sight hounds will course and kill a small dog, but probably do not realise until the deed is done that their quarry is one of their own species, having been impelled by their instinctive reaction, on seeing a small animal in motion ahead, to regard it as quarry. Other dogs may kill in the course of defence those which intrude on their territory, the prime cause of street dog fights in days gone by. A few dogs, specially 'entered' to aggression and encouraged in it, kill by intent any dog unfortunate enough to confront them. But dogs in general do not commit murder, and indeed their code of conduct includes the procedure for surrender and acceptance of surrender to which reference has already been made.

At the less violent level dogs have an evident sense of loyalty, and perhaps a rudimentary conscience. The demeanour of a dog which knows it has done wrong is familiar and needs no description. The point of interest is that often this demeanour is the first indication to its master that the dog has in fact done wrong. The attitude, expression and behaviour of contrition has not in those instances been assumed because the dog has been reprimanded, but because of its own knowledge that a crime has been committed. Dogs certainly have a sense of gratitude. Though never taught to do so, some of my own dogs do not fail to come to me after feeding in order to give the nose touch sign on taking leave. I assume it a recognition that the pack leader stands at that moment in the guise of provider.

More to the point, in the context of gundog training, is the evidence that the canine mind is constantly absorbent, taking in new knowledge of the ways of game; forming new sequences of action and reaction, some being helpful and others harmful to the functions the dogs must perform; acquiring new habits, good and bad. The inference for the trainer is of the need for constant vigilance – not only to nip in the bud contact which will be detrimental to gundog work, but to seize every opportunity of capitalising on those chance occurrences which may be used to extend it.

It often seems that these chance occurrences teach a lesson more efficiently than a formal training session can do. This, anyway, has been my impression and is perhaps explained by the probability that the mere fact of the happening having taken place has sensitised the dog's mind to the sequel. Further, I do not believe that a formal training session is necessarily the best sensitiser. Some dogs are always ready to accept instruction; they are enviable possessions, for the quality of co-operation makes life easier, but they are not always strong on brains. Other dogs regard the panoply of instruction – the evidence of whistle, leads and bags of dummies – with unconcealed boredom and in consequence learn little from the occasion; they are generally the intelligent ones. Among dogs, as with men, possessors of intelligence are seldom those most easily dealt with.

8

THE BIRTHRIGHTS

The great drives of energy which purpose-bred gundogs inherit, and which trainers must control and channel so that they operate in ways which serve the purposes of modern sportsmen, take two forms. The first is the hunting instinct. Since we also possess it, there is no difficulty in understanding this. It is the compulsion to be up and doing, to go out in search of those things which magnetise our attention, to quest and probe, surmounting or penetrating all obstacles to our desire, feeling that heightened energisation which its fulfilment creates, enlarging ourselves by feeling our speed and agility and stamina lifting us above the limitations which apply to those less adequate than ourselves.

These things can be shared by all sportsmen with their gundogs. What we cannot share with them is their extra heady onset of exhilaration which is the effect on gundogs of live-game scent, acting on them as does the horn to a foxhound or the trumpet to a soldier. What they cannot share with us is our knowledge of the sporting conventions and tactical considerations under which this overpowering enthusiasm is to be employed. The presence of game birds, wildfowl, hares and rabbits, and of the gun itself can and do excite to fever pitch those dogs which inherited their awareness from long lines of ancestry. But to be useful to Man, and satisfying to the dogs them-selves, these flows of energy must be guided towards helpful objectives and held in check until required.

Here the other form of canine desire is our chief aid. This is the ambition which all dogs possess in some degree, but gundogs more than any, to be of service to the human companions whom they accept as their pack leaders. It is easy to deduce how this urge to serve – absent from the wolf, the fox and the wild dog – became a component of the character of domestic dogs, and why it should be so dominant an urge in gundogs.

Obviously it anteceded any conscious breeding for particular purposes, though this in itself had been involuntarily progressing for many thousands of years before pedigrees were recorded. Archaeology has established that

Man and his dogs evolved together, sharing the camps and cave-homes of the Stone Ages. Even then the dogs-about-the-place would have been of service in different ways, their continued presence being tolerated for that reason alone. Those which did not justify themselves by doing something useful would not have lived long in human company. Their food was what they could scavenge in the human environment, and food was too valuable and hard to come by for even the offal to become the perquisite of hangers-on who contributed nothing to the camp's communal needs. The useless were expelled or killed; at least their pelts would clothe children. The useful would be integrated into the design for living; and the very useful would become part of the family.

Then, as now, they would have different functions. There would be hunting dogs, guards dogs and, later, herding dogs. The guard dogs would be fierce and powerful. They would not merely warn off, but physically repel or destroy, predatory animal intruders and human enemies. Their place would be outside the camp or cave, as is the place of huskies round Eskimo villages to this day. The herding dogs would be with the flocks and herds. But the hunting dogs, having helped in the chase and capture of the meal, would be included in the family circle, albeit on its fringe. We may be sure that in primitive times the returning hunters would have tales to tell of what their dogs had done, of their prowess and uncanny intelligence, and that these tales would grow in the telling, as they do now.

Not only would the man–dog link have started thus, but so also would that long ancestry, spanning the epochs, which has concentrated the hunting instinct and the serving instinct into the gundogs of today. The better a dog hunted and served, the more of a favourite it would become, the nearer the centre of the circle, and the greater its privileges. Because they shared the same ambience, favourite would mate with favourite; and because the bitch was a favourite, she would be allowed to rear her puppies. Now we have the products of that process which started so long ago, has been progressively intensified ever since, and has culminated in the pedigree registration systems of modern times. It is not, of course, wholly exclusive to gundogs. But the gundogs of today, the trainer's raw material, reflect that far-away past, and all that has happened in the way of evolution between then and now is significant in making the canine material on which we work less raw than at first we believe it to be. Compare the vision of the primitive camp fire man–dog partnership of distant ages with our own sporting version of their food procurement effort.

For me, one of the high moments of a covert shoot is the emergence of the beaters at the end of the first drive. Those fraught seconds between the appearance of the line of cheerful country faces at the edge of a wood, and the whistle or horn which signals 'All out', is akin to the parading of the cast at the end of a pantomime. At last, as it were, one can see who everybody is. Not least the dogs. Most of them will be recognisable as gundogs. Retrievers and spaniels predominate, each individual striving to give the impression of having done most of the work. Perhaps a German pointer will emerge, wearing that superior expression inseparable from the pointing breeds when temporarily caught up in less refined activities. Generally there will be at least one definite odd-dog-out.

A beagle, perhaps, thanks to precedents set in America; a border collie having a day off from herding sheep; a police German Shepherd Dog, moonlighting from constabulary duty; a King Charles spaniel, proclaiming that all is not yet lost of the original family spirit; a dachshund; I have even seen a Pekinese in the line, and he was no passenger. Almost certainly there will be a short-legged terrier, standing there regaining his breath, muddied, modest, and a little cocky, like a scrum-half at half time in a rugby match.

Though conventional gundogs are obviously more likely to be good at the job of pushing out (or 'bushing' in gamekeeping jargon), ancestral aptitudes being added to a greater expectation of opportunity, there is no limit on other volunteers. All that is asked in the beating line is that dogs should do what is useful, be under control, and avoid social gaffes such as barking in polite company. For this, terriers of the Jack Russell or hunt type have much to offer, if fit, brave and sensible. Not every such terrier is all or any of these things. Some are excitable little hooligans, some are wet little softies. But those which have what it takes are ornaments to the scene – indeed to many scenes. They can claim to be dogs for all seasons, but mostly for the winter. Any of them which are sufficiently versatile may have the chance of flushing pheasants, unseating rabbits, turning their paws to a spot of ferreting, executing rats and, of course, going down to fox. Such a one is not likely to be the bombastic sort. Most probably he will look a little sober-sided, which is all to the good in enterprises which require something more than impulsiveness.

The question which arises periodically of what is the best type of terrier for these varied functions reflects directly back on to gundog breeding, so let us pursue it further. My answer, as with all other working dogs, is 'the one that will do the job'. It is more than a simple matter of handsome is as handsome does, however, because the all-round, unregistered sporting terrier offers a valuable case history.

A movement to secure recognition of the 'breed' by the Kennel Club has existed for many years. Generally it has been sporadic, catching on for a few years under the impetus of some dedicated enthusiasts, then flickering out. Recently it has been pressed home by some able and energetic people. Whether it succeeds or not is neither here nor there to most sporting terrier owners. Among gundogs we have the example of, say, the English springer spaniel to establish that even though the Kennel Club Rules lay down (quite properly) that a 'standard' must be adopted for every recognised breed there is no need for all, or even a majority, of its devotees to conform to it. The 'standard', or specification of what the breed should look like, is for show-judging purposes alone. Only a minority of those who register their English springers at the Kennel Club are interested in shows. The same may well apply, and continue to apply, to another breed belatedly accorded recognition – the border collie, or working sheepdog.

In short, while those interested in exhibition awards are free to breed whatever they conceive to be the stipulated show type, those interested in other and more practical canine functions remain equally free to breed whatever type each of us prefers. The value of Kennel Club registration remains undiminished because the breeding of every type can then be authenticated, however disparate, as is already the case with spaniels.

Every owner of active dogs has his preferences. In terriers, mine is for a broken coat – harsh, dense, short enough not to be woolly, and long enough to lie cleanly along the contours of the body. Very essential is a neck which is both long, strong, and so set on that it seems to flow into the shoulders which, in all good-necked dogs, are likely to be well laid back. The reasons for the two latter points are operational, not cosmetic. Power and reach in the neck permits maximum pick-up ability when ratting, and that quick wrench which instantly kills the rat. Properly raked shoulders are necessary for a dog which, when working underground to fox, may be able to about-turn only by somersaulting within its own length. A stuffy little short-necked, straight-shoulders terrier has no hope of doing this, and its owner's proud tales of sporting derring-do can be taken with a pinch of salt.

The varied composition of the canine element in a shooting party, including the presence of non-gundogs in a gundog role, has its application to the specialised question of breeding and training for this limited purpose. It raises the question, fundamental to the preservation of inherited aptitudes and operational efficiency, of the relative values of recorded ancestry and fidelity to type. The Kennel Club, a much abused and often unfairly abused institution, deals in both. It rightly claims to serve the interests of all who possess pedigree dogs, whatever those interests are.

Prominent among them is the show interest. Since few breeds outside the gundog group now perform the function for which they were evolved, dog-showing is much the preponderant element in the Club's administrative activity, and as a source of revenue. The judging of dogs in the show ring is on the basis of written breed standards; how they are written, and how they are interpreted, being generally as important as the quality of the dogs to which they are applied, and sometimes more important. However, there is no need for dogs registered at the Kennel Club to conform to the standards of their particular breed, unless they are intended to be show dogs. Those bred to be gundogs are obviously not so intended, except in the hands of a diminishing number of enthusiasts who espouse both interests.

Gundogs bred to be used as gundogs, and not for anatomical comparison, can still be registered by the Kennel Club, whose registration system constitutes an irreplaceable record in complete detail of the genealogy of the dogs of the past century. Since ancestry is the paper expression of inherited ability, we are thus led back to the importance of pedigree and the non-importance of breed standards in relation to purpose-bred, active-service gundogs.

The facts support the following proposition: 'Any livestock to which a breed standard is applied thereafter functionally degenerates.' Among dogs, examples are too numerous for more than a few to be given here. The Great Dane was once a boar hound; it no longer sustains hunting pace and is geriatric at nine years old, at which age gundogs may have some seasons of work ahead of them (how long before the otterhound, now a show dog, reaches the same state?). The mastiff was a war dog before it was first a guard dog, then a show dog; now a mile walk is all it can take (how long before the show version of the border collie begins to lose its mobility?). Dandie Dinmont and Skye terriers were earth dogs once (how long before the Glen of Imaal joins them among the merely decorative?).

In breeds to which the standard is applied by some breeders for show purposes, but not by others who breed for work, the contrast between the theoretical and the practical proclaims its own comment. Show prizes go to English setters too heavy-headed for proper balance, and so having a lumbering gait when questing, in contrast to the true skimming gallop of working setters; to basset hounds which sink on plough; to bulldogs which are their own health hazards from birth. The breed standard may well be a design, albeit outdated, for an operational animal. The same cannot be said, however, for the interpretation of it by breeders and judges. Did terrier men of an older day ever intend the modern appearance of the Kerry Blue terrier, or of the Sealyham? I do not disparage either; equally, nobody can say that their show-ring modern versions are those of practical terriers.

The inevitability of degeneration when a breed standard demands the halting of evolution is confirmed by what has happened in other forms of livestock. For speed, endurance and intelligence the racing pigeon is one of the wonders of Man-adapted Nature. A century ago pigeon shows (which have a longer history than dog, horse or agricultural shows) scheduled classes for them. Most pigeon-racers continued to breed for flying power but a minority sought glory in the show-pen. After a few generations the birds of families which were not raced, but had been bred to the breed standard, inevitably degenerated; their descendants exist now as that pleasantly grotesque fancy breed officially known as the carrier pigeon. The standard which had done the damage was first amended, then replaced.

The new standard was defined as being for 'show homers'. These in due course also degenerated, so that a third breed standard for 'exhibition homers' had to be drawn up. The end of the road is not necessarily in sight. The lesson also applies to horse and pony, and farm livestock. Here the developments form the same chain of cause and effect. Try viewing them from the opposite direction.

The Apaloosa is not sought after to win races, show-jumping, or events. It is merely spotted, a kind of equine Dalmatian – both cases in which appearance has superseded performance as a *raison d'etre*. The shorthorn lost its prime place among dairy cattle when over-attention to awards in the show ring led to under-attention to what was going into the bucket. Basic poultry breeds of the inter-war years – Wyandottes, Orpingtons, Minorcas, Light Sussex – have become rarities because what they look like is now regarded as less important than what they produce – not as important, as it used to be.

So breed standards, though essential in the short term for the showing of livestock, eventually undermine the breeds to which they apply by causing breeding objectives to be retrospective to the date when the standard was decided, and hence inhibiting the improvement in type as well as performance which equates with evolution by natural selection. The process, of course, is slow. Breeds as a whole degenerate over periods; every individual in them does not degenerate at the same time. Some strains are protected by the cordon sanitaire of breeding specifically for performance, and excluding from future generations the influence of non-performers, however closely they may be held to fulfil the breed standard. In all livestock, even in their most rigidly utilitarian strains, some are bred which will not hunt, face cover, go to earth, retrieve, fly home, give milk, gain weight, gallop, or whatever their function is. They are not bred from, to the improvement of the generations to come.

The way to improve a function is to ensure that only the best performers at it contribute to the future, and that the failures do not; in other words, breeding always from the top-performance layer. Unfortunately, the risk exists in some gundog breeds, where the idea of 'dual purpose' persists, that second-rate performers may be used for breeding because they fulfil the requirements of the breed standard. Immediately the principle of natural selection, through progeniture only by the most able, is diluted. The breed standard has done its deadly work again.

Since the pedigree represents the extent to which the dog that bears it can be expected to embody the two priceless birthrights of the born gundog, the instinct to hunt and readiness to serve its master, it becomes a very meaningful document. It also becomes susceptible to misinterpretation, misrepresentation and, in rare instances, falsification. In former times the latter could be, and was, perpetrated by the unscrupulous with an easy mind. He who was sold a pup had, in the fullest sense of the term, bought it; and that was that. Recent legislation has altered this situation for the better. However, it is still desirable for those who buy gundogs to be aware of potential pitfalls.

The Kennel Club itself became aware of some of them as a result of study-ing the effect of the Trade Descriptions Act. It amended certain of its technicalities relating to awards in gundog trials and shows in order to remove ambiguities. Even so, legislation has not removed the principle of *caveat emptor* (let the buyer beware). It is still up to buyers of gundogs to watch their own interests. They may do so more effectively if they know how some of the terms used in advertisements, sales letters and sales talk may be misconstrued, by accident or design. In the existing state of the law the examples to be quoted, and others like them, are more than semantics.

It is important to remember that the pedigrees supplied by breeders, generally for five or six generations, have no official force, though always accepted between men of goodwill. They are, in fact, memoranda drawn up for the convenience of the breeders themselves and their customers. But unofficial as they are, they may constitute breaches of the Act if they are inaccurate or couched in misleading terms. For instance the only 'titles' recognised by the Kennel Club for gundogs are in abbreviation FT Ch, Sh Ch and Ch, meaning Field Trial Champion, Show Champion and (full) Champion (i.e., a Show Champion which has passed a qualifying test at a field trial). An advertisement may state, say, '15 Champions in pedigree' without stipulating which categories of Champion. There is nothing in-accurate about this, but it could be misleading to the extent of allowing an inexperienced buyer or a foreigner seeking a shooting dog to acquire a show dog instead, or vice versa. This has happened to more than one spouse giving a present to wife or husband.

The official warrants of breeding are the registration certificates, which are the basis for the extended pedigrees which the Kennel Club supplies for an extra fee. Except in cases of export, or of material doubt, the latter are in practice regarded as superfluous, and the written unofficial breeders' pedigrees as sufficient. These can, of course, be verified by research into the Stud Books and Breed Record Supplements, but the labour is great. Unfortunately they can contain still more snags, of which examples follow.

To the officially recognised titles some breeders add another of their own on their pedigree sheets, the letters FTW, meaning field trial winner. Although this does not designate what category of trial has been won (e.g. as between Novice and Open), it may be thought all very well in its way so long as it does not mean less than it says. But this can happen. Some animals cited as FTW prove to have been the winners of working tests; these, being simulated, unrecognised, and using inanimate targets, are very different from field trials. Others have 'won' minor recognitions, such as Certificate of Merit, in field trials. Here the Kennel Club's long toleration of imprecise wording in its official records opened the door to misrepresentation. It was the Club's own practice until 1966 to record in the Stud Book every dog which achieved any field trial award as a 'winner' regardless of whether it had finished first or received one of half a dozen certificates.

Tradition dies hard. With this precedent, some dogs designated FTW in a breeder's pedigree prove (not necessarily to the knowledge of the immediate breeder, who may merely be repeating a designation handed down to him) to have in fact achieved no more than a certificate. This is not to denigrate certificates. The intention is to denigrate terms which can mislead. The Club was wise to have extended its corrective process. But not all newspaper and magazine staff have the technical knowledge to challenge advertisements which, even if in good faith, may be describing animals on offer in terms which express less or more than the precise truth.

The hazards multiply when the subject is extended to conversation. It is possible for a seller to say of a dog which has never had a bird shot to it 'He has had a certificate in a qualifying stake' (though we hope this does not occur often). To a shooting man with some knowledge of field trials these words could mean that the judges in a trial which qualifies dogs to run in a Championship (i.e. an Open or All-Aged stake colloquially known as 'a qualifier') gave the animal a certificate of merit – at that level, no mean award. But the words can also mean, official terminology being what it still is, that the dog, having won a Challenge certificate at a show, was granted a working certificate at a 'qualifying stake' in the sense that show dogs were allowed to take their test there to qualify them for the title of full Champion concurrently with the running of a trial of which they were not part – circumstances in which 'planted' dead birds have sometimes been used to test retrieving.

It is sad that misconstructions, of which the above are examples but not exhaustive, should ever be used in the course of a deal; sadder still that the way should be open for it to happen through the shortcomings of official verbiage. Though the Kennel Club did well to clear its lines as far as it did, it could have gone further. For instance, to cease categorising as 'field trials' what it also describes as 'specialist club qualifying trials' whereby dogs which have won awards in shows are tested at work. These are not, nor do they purport to be, field trials. Though the regulations stipulate that field trial judges shall officiate at them, they are not judged to field trial levels, nor are the competing dogs subject to field trial eliminating faults. Yet their inclusion in the field trial list could lead a vendor offering a dog which gained an award at one of them to describe it as having a field trial award, and it would also preclude legal sanctions against what would be, at the very least, a major misunderstanding.

From this it will be seen that pedigrees in whatever form are more than family histories, and very much more than curiosity value. Their significance can be both under-estimated and over-estimated. Those who under-estimate them discount the essential fact that the pedigree indicates how concentrated a degree of gundog birthright could have been transmitted by the ancestors of the animals they contemplate buying, or using for breeding. A pedigree is no more a 'fad' or a 'frill', as such people sometimes describe it, than are the specifications of a motor car. Admittedly some knowledge is needed to assess a pedigree fully, and it is here that the over-estimators can leave themselves vulnerable. A pedigree can never be a guarantee, yet some people behave as if it were, discussing genetic fusions, combinations and permutations until the pedigree becomes almost more important than the dog.

Perhaps the lessons are that the dog one likes is the dog to have, provided that the evidence of birthright is solid; but the dog one likes is not the dog to have if the birthright has been diluted by the infusion of animals which have not passed the performance tests of work. This does not necessarily mean field trial awards; there are gundogs which have never come under the judges but are as capable as any field triallers, but it is essential to know them by personal observation over a period, rather than to rely on reported reputations, which may have become inflated. Where field trial awards are of incontrovertible value is that they prove a dog which one has never seen to have passed a searching, sometimes harsh, test in the essentials of its work, including those aspects not perceptible from a distance such as 'mouth' and freedom from whine.

The problems which beset those gundogs in whom the working birthrights have become diluted are well exemplified by the case of the minor spaniel breeds. There is now no point in challenging English springers in competition with any other breed. Occasionally a cocker, of which there are many excellent exponents in their own specialised and different sphere, can share the money with them; so, less frequently, can Welsh springers, Clumbers, Sussex and Irish water spaniels. But in general the supremacy of the English springer among spaniels is as great as that of the thoroughbred among horses, and for anything else to oppose them is not, in bridge terms, a business bid.

However, this has not deterred enthusiasts from making the attempt to rehabilitate the long redundant working capacities of what have become termed the minor spaniel breeds. The first problem confronting them is one of investigation to locate the working qualities diffused by generations of breeding from show-winning stock, in which the working capacity has gone unmonitored. The Welsh springer spaniel poses fewer problems than others, because large numbers of the breed have always been worked, including many of its show dogs. The modern breed has earned a high reputation for thoroughness, courage and stamina in working heavy cover; but few recommendations for biddability and mouth; in short latterly a breed with one birthright but not the other. To remedy this deficiency the breed club has been organising 'shooting days' at which working qualities can be assessed, to the great benefit of breeders planning future matings. Welsh springers have the advantage of being able to match the hunting abilities of English springers. Other minor breeds are less fortunate in this respect, their problems correspondingly greater. Though both breeds have gained awards in all-breed stakes during recent seasons, how can a water spaniel rival the cover-penetration of a springer or cocker, or a Clumber match their tempo? Both must wait for conditions so overwhelmingly unfavourable that nose and nose alone decides the issue, and then hope that their noses are the best present on the day.

9

Tracing the Inheritance

The inherited urges to hunt and to serve divided long since into several streams, mixing in varied proportions, and it is diverse mixtures which distinguish from each other the characters of the three categories of gundog. The pointer-retrievers are omitted at this stage, not in disparagement, but because, being a combination of two existing categories, their special nature came about after the fusion took place. For the moment we consider pointers and setters, spaniels, and retrievers.

Only the retrievers were specifically evolved for working to the gun. Our native setters and spaniels, originating as the same breed but separately developed to perform different functions over the past five hundred years, had been helping falconers and fowlers for centuries before guns were invented, let alone used in sport. The setting dogs, later joined by the pointers which cáme of different ancestry on the European mainland, located the game at which falcons and hawks were flown, refraining from flushing it until ordered to do so after the falcons had been cast off and had reached a height from which they could stoop on their prey. Spaniels, hunting more closely and often in woodland too thick for falcons to be flown, flushed their game immediately into nets which had been set previously. There was no use for a specialist retrieving dog until less than a century and a half ago; until, in fact, a technical advance created one.

When every game gun was a muzzle-loader the re-loading process took so long that there could be no likelihood of more than three or four birds being on the ground simultaneously for any one Gun. There was also the certainty of ample time in which they could be found by man or dog, before the party would wish to move on. Retrieving was a secondary function, assumed to be within the compass of every gundog worth the name, albeit at the modest standard to which retrieving was then performed. General Hutchinson, whose *Dog Breaking* was the first standard work on the subject, makes no mention of it as a separate breed-function in his original edition in 1848; nine re-editions were to follow in the next half-century, by which time retrieving had become the prime necessity in the opinion of most sportsmen wealthy enough to shoot driven game.

The change was a by-product of breech-loading, which also changed the nature of game-shooting and its participants. It made re-loading so rapid that Guns could fire and fire again at birds driven over them, fast enough to deal with a flush of pheasants, or with two or more large coveys of partridges arriving only seconds apart. Many more birds were thereafter on the ground at any one time. Not only were greater numbers to be found and collected, but the difficulty of keeping track of runners was both complicated and multiplied.

Equally far-reaching changes affected the human element, and their attitude. Instead of the shooter having to go to the game, the game could now be brought to the shooter. So the prototype shooter was no longer an active countryman, the extent of whose opportunity depended on the excellence of his questing dogs, the use of his legs, and the skilful application of his own fieldcraft and knowledge of Nature. Instead the trends were set by those who could afford to be at their pegs, from which they had small need to move, except to go to other pegs as drive followed drive. The introduction of money as a qualification for being in a shooting party, often superseding the operational competence which had previously been the decisive factor, raised the average age and limited the mobility of the participants. To be well enough endowed to pay one's way at driven game came most easily to those with their professional or business careers behind them, rather than in front. Their kind of shooting was a stationary sport, because in the main they were stationary men. All that most of them wanted to see of dog-work was the game coming back to them in retrievers' mouths, a prospect which pleased them mightily, since it redounded by implication to their own glory. A dog which could find and bring to them a dead bird was esteemed more highly than one which could find and flush a live one in such a manner that it could be shot. In no way to their discredit, but as a matter of fact, these reduced-participation sportsmen excluded themselves, or were excluded, from aspects of a shooting day which had previously been part and parcel of it – the provision, locating, and presentation of the game. These operations were increasingly left to keepers and beaters. At its highest levels game-shooting had become less of a sport in which men pitted their wits against the quarry and exercised their hunting instincts, and more a form of entertainment.

Latterly, of course, the trend has reversed. Cost factors, and the reduced rural labour pool, limit the recruitment of beaters. Dogs are resuming their original functions. There are other changes for the better. The emergence of pickers-up and dog-handlers as participant sportsmen and sportswomen in their own roles, and the value of well-trained dogs in replacing the missing human element, have greatly strengthened and broadened the interest in game shooting in its modern guise. At the same time the revival of those forms of shooting which depend on the man (as well as the dog) having a hunting instinct is evident. A consequence was the rapid relative upsurge in working spaniels *vis-à-vis* working retrievers, in the comparable resurgence in working pointers and setters, and to the appearance and growth on the British scene of the pointer-retrievers, formerly confined to mainland Europe.

However, none of these things alters the fact that the introduction of the breech loader at about the end of the Crimean War resulted in an immediate demand for specialist retrievers, and that the breeds which then emerged still exist unchanged. They were produced by combining the newly imported labrador with the blood of native British gundogs. The efficient and stylish retrievers of today are evidence of what selective breeding, knowledgeably applied, has created in a century and a half.

There is little documentation of how that evolution was achieved, despite its far-reaching significance for one of our major sports. But what can be deduced throws interesting light on the share-out of the heritage on which gundog work and training is based. Retriever work demands that the exercise of the drive to hunt must be delayed until after the shooting has taken place. It must therefore be subservient in the dog's psychological make-up to the drive to serve. Spaniel work, by contrast, demands that the dog shall find its game twice – both before and after the shot is fired. First the questing spaniel seeks out and flushes the bird or moves the rabbit so that it becomes airborne or visible where it can be shot; if game falls the spaniel is sent out to find it and bring it to hand. Of the two the first find is the more important, because unless game is found there will be no shooting, and the matter of retrieving will not arise.

In making the initial find, a spaniel is sent out with no positive knowledge that game is in the area, whereas the retriever has the indication, from the fact of a shot having been fired, that a definite task awaits him. The spaniel therefore needs his inherited drives in reverse priority, the hunting instinct being more essential than the serving instinct. The finding of unshot game will more often depend on his initiative than on his regard for orders; spaniel temperament is therefore more vehement than retriever temperament.

Not only is, but ought to be. If the reasons for it are born in mind the often heard supposition that spaniels are 'wilder' than retrievers can be seen in perspective. The truth is not that they are less controllable, but less controlled. Forgetful of the basic urges, some people expect spaniels to become satisfactory shooting dogs if trained in the same manner as retrievers – and, though less frequently, vice versa. Knowledge of the unseen characteristics of the raw material is essential to the production of gundogs, as it is to any other productive enterprise. The difference between retrievers and spaniels is not in the visible factors of appearance, length of coat, or amount of space needed in a car (matters which seem to exercise the minds of some people when deciding the acquisition of a gundog), but in what the animal will be required to do, and in the relative strength of its inborn motivating forces.

The same order of priorities, with a modification, applies to the pointing breeds. They operate in a different element. Retrievers and spaniels are concerned with the ground on which we also stand and move, and with the cover which we also can see. Bird dogs are primarily concerned with the air, preferably in the form of wind, but with all its movements however slight, its eddies however labyrinthine. Moreover their moments of truth occur when they are remote from their handlers, perhaps hundreds of yards away. Therefore, for reasons of distance and the fact that they operate in an element largely outside our own perceptions, they are less subject to 'handling' in the sense of tactical influence while they are working. In their case not only is the drive to hunt their dominating impulse, but it is something which training can do little to enhance. All a trainer can do is to shape the heritage which ancestry has bequeathed to each dog.

The mixing of inherited urges and aptitudes has formed the canine minds on which gundog trainers work, varying from breed to breed according to the special function for which each has been evolved. These variations of character, and the responses – to command and to temptation alike – which knowledgeable trainers expect to result from them, reduce the element of unknown quantity in the training process, and shape the manner in which this should be planned. There being considerable overlap in the theoretical functions of retrievers and spaniels, consider what the mixing of the drives means in practice.

Down from the Dark Ages has come the continual moulding of the two components in spaniel nature. First, the compulsive hunting instinct, refined by a remarkable power – sometimes apparent as early as six weeks old – to discriminate between the scents of game and rabbits and those of less interesting creatures; secondly, the spaniel's almost notorious capacity for hero-worship of the man or woman in its life, which unless sensibly kept in proportion can degenerate into sentimentality, perhaps on both sides. This is a hot and heady mixture, needing a deft touch in training if it is to be employed successfully. In comparison, the cooler nature of retrievers reflects their shorter history.

Where a spaniel worships, expressing its devotion in terms of action which are sometimes impulsive, a retriever is more soberly dutiful so long as the human partner remains suitably dominant. When the time came to create the retriever, which was evidently a conscious act by the sportsmen of the time, the preponderance of basic ancestry came from breeds which rendered a service to man. The most important was the long under-valued but now supreme labrador. Their history in Britain began when compact, short-coated dogs with extra-special swimming powers caught the eyes of the then Earl of Malmesbury and the perspicacious Colonel Radclyffe, a Dorset squire, in the 1850s on the quayside of Poole and other southern English ports where Portuguese timber boats unloaded their cargoes from the North American forests. In Portuguese the word 'labrador' meant, and still means 'workman' – the useful dog. It implied no connection with the territory on Canada's north-eastern seaboard which is now called Labrador, but was not then. Both these gentlemen perceived the value of such dogs in the sport of shooting. Both thereafter pioneered their breeding here. The graveyard of the grand originals of English labradors still exists, well guarded, on the present Earl's estate. Both the Malmesbury and the Radclyffe names remain potent forces in labrador pedigrees, with their heritage of robust physiques and high intelligence adapted to the shooting scene.

Nor is it likely that the dogs we know as labradors originated anywhere in the New World. Almost certainly they were as Iberian as their masters, sharing with them the transatlantic voyages of the timber ships and fishing boats, constantly playing their part by leaping into the sea and bringing back whatever slid overboard, such as blocks, spars, ropes, floats, fenders, and of course fish accidentally swept away by waves when nets were being worked in rough weather. Their descendants reflect this ancestry. Breed for breed, gundog or otherwise, no dog swims as well, nor in the same manner, as labradors.

The shooting men of Britain took half a century to realise the true worth of what many at first regarded as Colonel Radclyffe's private enthusiasm. Chauvinistic as sportsmen often are, they could not believe that a ready-made retriever was waiting to be used, or that any gundog could be evolved for the new purpose in hand unless it possessed in its ancestry the blood of our traditional working breeds. But they were wise enough to use the labrador as an ingredient. With the black setters of Ireland and the Western Isles as base, and infusions of labrador, Gordon setter and collie (to give biddability), they produced the elegant flatcoat, which remained the most popular retriever until the turn of the century. Second to it was the curlycoat, with the Irish water spaniel and the standard poodle as bases. Much later came the golden retriever, founded on a strain of water spaniels from Tweeddale and infusions of collie blood. By that time the intrinsic worth of the labrador pure and simple was recognised; the flatcoat supremacy was reversed within ten years, the first decade of the twentieth century; the curly-coat never rose above minority level; despite enormous popularity as a show dog, the golden has never challenged the labrador as a worker except through a few specialised working strains led by that of Mrs J. R. Atkinson of Holway in Dorset.

More detailed advance knowledge of the strengths and weaknesses, chief aptitudes and ways of working which may be expected from any given ancestry is of obvious help to a trainer. Though it is true that when considering the finished products we assess them on the principle that a good retriever is a good retriever (in other words, one that delivers the good regardless of colour, sex, size or breed), the same animal in its emergent stages may seem very different. To be watching for its inherited tendencies to develop is much better than learning them by hindsight.

Labradors take life more seriously when young than the other retriever breeds. They are willing learners, gaining positive satisfaction from the knowledge that they are approved of. This degree of co-operation in labradors is formally implanted as early as nine or ten months, but is generally deferred until twelve or fifteen months in golden retrievers, and to eighteen months or later in flatcoats. It varies slightly in character. The labrador, while not servile, is the perfect servant to those whom he respects, though as ready as any other gundog to run wild if allowed to. The golden is more of a friend, depending more heavily on a heart-to-heart relationship than on an accepted code of discipline. The flatcoat is likewise a companion rather than an employee, with an exuberant side to his nature which presents a special problem; if crushed, as it can be, a very dull dog results; if contained, as it also can be, a particularly attractive comradeship can be built up. But the flatcoat's inherent exuberance and sometimes mistimed sense of humour are lifelong characteristics, and leave him, even in old age, occasionally prey to the playboy touch.

Distant ancestry stamps its mark on all four breeds. The greater element of setter blood in the flatcoat's make-up is both his strength and weakness, being the root cause of his swift supersession by the labrador eighty years ago, and his position as the third breed in modern retriever field trial ranking. His 'nose' is demonstrably the most sensitive, giving him 'touches' at several yards' further range than others. But what he does with the touches is compromised by the exciteability which comes of setter ancestry, and with it an instinctive reaction to rely on effort, movement and energy rather than on painstaking thoroughness. He relies on his legs rather than his brains, and though unsurpassed as a game-finder, he covers a great deal of ground in finding it. This characteristic of flatcoats tells us, by comparison, something of value about labradors and goldens.

Nothing short of many more generations of careful breeding will eliminate the setter element from the flatcoat's hunting style. It is there for all to see. The wide, swinging pattern orientating on the wind, the recurrent high head searching for body-scent, the sweeping of the ground as distinct from hunting it closely then gradually closing the range on a 'touch' all bespeak the airiness of setter work. The contrast with the labrador is revealing. The labrador hunts small areas closely, its nose constantly down, criss-crossing on its previous course and continually turning, plaiting its movements together and giving itself the benefit of varied angles on the wind. If this process is watched in cover which gives full visibility, such as sugar beet, an irresistible vision is created. It is that of a dog which is not working on land at all, but swimming – twisting and searching for some object made elusive by choppy waters. The labrador's long-ago role in human service was precisely that.

If it is argued that many golden retrievers do similarly, as is indeed the case, is not this precisely the terrestrial version of what a waterborne dog does when questing for a duck, as was the function of water spaniels on Tweed-side and elsewhere?

The need with labradors and goldens is to teach them to apply their close-hunting techniques to the areas where the lost game is most likely to be lying; in short, to work to signal. The readiness with which labradors acquire this skill is alone enough to explain their supremacy in field trials. It enables their hunting power to be deployed effectively and quickly, and the game to be recovered with minimum disturbance to unshot birds lying in the vicinity with which the shooting party hope to deal later. The problem for the trainer of a flatcoat is to contain the scope of the ground coverage, concentrating it to the locations where it is likely to be useful. He will be a good man if he succeeds, but it can be done; and, when, it is done, a dog of exceptional capability results.

Inherited characteristics, of which the foregoing are examples, are invariably two-sided. It may be said that every gundog weakness is a strength which has become uncontrolled. The contrast between the most popular two working breeds of spaniel, springer and cocker, makes the point. How two breeds of evident common ancestry, and known to have been much inter-bred in the past two centuries, can differ so markedly in character is one of the exceptions which are said to prove rules.

The springer, athletic, high couraged yet mild in temperament, is as strongly predisposed towards human partnership as any breed of gundog; perhaps, in the case of some of the most carefully bred and purely working strains, more strongly than any others. He has his faults, inevitably. But these are almost always faults of over-enthusiasm, comparatively rarely are they faults of rebellion. The cocker, equally deeply committed to the end-products of his task, combines great abilities with a steely self-will and, when he sees fit, a contempt for all humanity. One way of putting the distinction is that springers can be taught, but cockers learn. Where they gain knowledge can only be experience, fused on to an inherited receptivity. No breed of dog is more effective in exploiting the Nelson touch than the working cocker, and it is in turning a blind eye and deaf ear to orders that they do some of their most successful work.

Whereas the springer subordinates his thinking to the will of his master, the cocker stiffly maintains his independence (while not above making a great show of devotion for diplomatic reasons). It seems that in consequence the cocker goes on thinking his own thoughts and storing up his conclusions, throughout his life, extending his game sense with every passing season, building up new skills even when his age is in double figures. Tough-minded, durable in body, immensely strong for his size, the cocker is a formidable combination of qualities in his own scope and in his own way – if only he can be controlled. It is his readiness to ignore orders and act on the evidence of his senses that makes the cocker the best of all spaniels in retrieving strong runners, and perhaps the equal of specialist retrievers in this important work. Once fairly on a line his bottomless determination is proof against anything that may deflect him, including human efforts to help or even recall him, until the bird is in his mouth.

Again allowance for these differences governs the design of training programmes. It also explains why some of the most gifted professionals excel with springers and others with cockers, though to the superficial observer there may seem no great difference between the breeds. In fact there are several differences. For all-round purposes the springer is undoubtedly the superior, being always an optimist and therefore adaptable. The cocker, by nature a realist, is inclined to pessimism when things are not to his liking. In face of a known difficulty, a cocker has the heart of a lion, but he is no enthusiast for forlorn hopes, and if asked to beat out a gameless piece of country is apt to treat the proposition with the contempt it deserves. Most obviously, perhaps, a springer at four years old has revealed the level of performance he will maintain through life. A cocker learns more slowly but continues learning, and will still be improving and approaching his peak at eight or nine.

Among the pointer breeds the countries of origin have left their mark. The pointer, as Iberian in origin as the labrador and with a known ancestry extending much further back into Time, shares the same characteristics, confirming the probability of some degree of common ancestry. The best pointers are, in human idiom, wrapped up in their work – responsible, painstaking, sensible, with no great levity when off-duty. English setters have basic common ground with springer spaniels – an eternal optimism in questing, great *élan* in performance, their whole attitude demonstrating dash and pleasure in what they do.

Gordon setters suggest something of the traditional dour Scot in their make-up; one senses that few 'soft' dogs survived in the past to contribute to the make-up of the present generation; and one sees, with no cause for doubt, that a good Gordon in hands strong enough to merit his respect is unsurpassed among bird dogs for skills and stamina. The Irish setters – the latterly popular reds having fortunately been rejoined by the almost extinct but now revitalised white-and-reds – work with the never-say-die spirit of Ireland. There, in the track of incoming Atlantic storms, game populations were never high. On those grouse moors hours may pass, and many miles be covered, between finds. Generations in which endless effort met with rare rewards gave no place to faint hearts and endowed the modern Irish setters with inexhaustible bodies and minds.

Such generalisations as these must be combined with another all-important truth about gundog behaviour, reactions, and performance. It is that variations are as great between strains within a breed as they are between one breed and another of the same group. It is obvious that there will be distinctive character patterns as between, say, any retriever and any spaniel. What is not so obvious is that the contrasts between two particular strains of labrador may be as wide as those between labradors as a whole and goldens as a whole. The same applies to strains within the springer and cocker breeds, the various setters and the pointer, the German pointer-retrievers and Munsterlanders, Weimaraners and vizslas.

Buying or breeding gundogs is like buying or blending wine. The name of the breed equates with the *appellation* label on the bottle. To know what to expect of the contents of the bottle one needs also to know the vineyard which produced it, and the year in which it did so. That question, so often asked, 'Where can I buy a good springer?' is as impossible to answer as

'Where can I buy a good bottle of Burgundy?' It is a matter of taste or requirement. What kind of springer? Which sort of Burgundy? The preference of the owner-to-be is relevant in each case. So is the purpose intended. Only if these are known can a suitable purchase be arranged. When buying, or beginning the training of a gundog, it is essential to look ahead, visualising the work it will be called upon to do, and matching its in-built inherited characteristics to it.

At first hearing, the term covert-shooting implies a rather formal, socially smooth occasion; rough-shooting, in contrast, suggests an opportunistic, unplanned, take-what-comes foray. This is not the whole truth, and where dog-work is concerned only a very small fraction of the truth. Underlying outward appearances, the essential difference between rough-shooting and any form of driven-game is that the former includes the element of hunt, which in the latter is dismissed as a job for the infrastructure. Rough-shooters rely on their fieldcraft, knowledge of the quarry, and above all on their dogs, to find the game and put it where they can shoot it. Driven-game shooters rely on beaters to put the game over their heads.

To compare the two is pointless. There is no superiority, only preferences. Their objectives are different. A man who seeks much shooting would regard rough-shooting as giving him too few opportunities to fire his gun. Others, who prefer that their bag should reflect their own efforts instead of being the end product of somebody else's organisation, are less happy sitting on sticks at covert side than when mobile behind a dog.

In rough-shooting the dog-work must be at its most efficient. There is no human element to replace it. The dog is as important as the gun. This is no disparagement of polished retrievers which sit, alert but poised, through the hottest drives, marking the falls and awaiting their orders. The best of them are magnificent of their kind. But the burr-encrusted, muddied and often very wet gundogs of many breeds which emerge from the depths of bramble clumps are not all rough-and-ready, hit-or-miss bush-busters. Unless at least some of them are better than that, there will not be much shooting, rough or otherwise.

To the untrained eye, dog-work at a rough shoot may indeed suggest a whole-hearted, press-on-regardless expenditure of effort, rather like Irishmen playing rugby football. In each case, appearances deceive. The Irishmen in all probability have nerves of ice, subtle brains, and a silken touch in smuggling out the ball at the tactically ideal time and place from what looks like a bar-room brawl. So with good rough-shooting dogs. Their work looks and sounds like a violent business, sometimes even crude. Dry sticks crackle, bramble is torn apart, dead willow-herb and nettle is demolished by some thrusting practitioner of what is actually a highly skilled function. A rough-shooting day's results depend on the game sense of the dogs, their gun sense, and their self-control in moments of pressure.

In a well-trained young dog still gaining experience, gun sense (which is an acquired skill) feeds upon game sense (which is largely inherited). Beginning from the realisation that the best place for a pheasant is in the air, and for a rabbit on open ground, there comes an awareness that the gun must also be given its best possible chance. In this respect 'working to the gun' is no mere picturesque phase. What the good rough-shooting dog soon develops, but which a driven-game dog needs in less degree, is a permanent communication system which lasts the whole of a shooting day. Through it the dog has a constant consciousness of the position of the shooter. By it, the shooter is constantly forewarned of what is about to happen – if he is able to 'read the dog'.

By its action, head carriage, the look in its eye, and above all by tail-action, a dog can give a running commentary on what its nose is telling it. The man who has prior indication that a pheasant is ahead, or that a rabbit is about to break, no longer has the element of surprise operating against him. A dog which merely evicts the quarry is only half a dog in rough-shooting terms. The other half of the dog, so to speak, is the shooter and the two must stay connected. These are among the finer points of gundog work which the dog and its master build up between themselves. The sense of mutual enterprise which results from them becomes the basis of those partnerships which men remember throughout their sporting lives.

This is a point at which the functions of retrievers and spaniels diverge in theory, but sometimes come together in practice. The purpose-bred questing dog for rough-shooting is the spaniel, the great all-rounder. The spaniel is to other gundogs what the commando soldier is to other troops – physically tireless, quick-thinking, resourceful, active, determined, self-reliant, adaptable, unstoppable by anything except his master's whistle. In short, the most versatile of all gundogs. He may well be called upon to climb rocks, burrow under fallen trees, swim rivers and jump forestry fencing all on the same day in pushing out game birds, and retrieving them when shot. Spaniels have no superiors at their range of skills. Whether they have equals for rough-shooting is debateable.

Some men, however, prefer retrievers for this work, believing them less demanding on the handler and for practical purposes as efficient. I would concede the former point; a spaniel with his blood up and game scent in his nose does indeed merit close attention: that is what he is there for, and it is beyond the capability of some sportsmen to give it. Just as not every foxhunter would be wholly happy riding to hounds on a thoroughbred (myself among them), there are shooters who prefer the less exciting but comparatively patent-safety retriever temperament, steadied by its extra ingredient of the instinct to serve. One cannot, however, rate retrievers as the equals of spaniels in what might be called the hard scrummaging of a dog in cover. But we are now less concerned with the qualities of dog versus dog, but with the effectiveness of man–dog partnerships. There are obviously man–retriever partnerships which are more effective than a man–spaniel partnership would be, given the same man.

There are two things, and two things only, at which modern retrievers excel modern spaniels. First they are undoubtedly more readily controlled by those who are not prepared, or not able, to keep half their minds constantly on the dog; secondly, they can be worked on unmarked retrieves at longer range. The things that a spaniel can do better than a retriever include putting birds on the wing and unseating rabbits, simply because they penetrate deeper cover and hunt it more thoroughly without the stimulus of a shot. Their ancestors were doing so long before there were shots to stimulate them; all the ancestors of retrievers were not.

This assertion will be disputed by some sincere admirers of retrievers. It is not to my advantage to be considered biased, so I have thought carefully before making it and as a result of that thought am convinced that it faithfully reflects what actually happens in sport. I have seen many pleasing demonstrations of hunting-up by labrador, golden and flatcoated retrievers. But demonstration is not always what it seems. The retrievers which go with such dash in front of a line of beaters are not always working the cover effectively; sometimes they are merely running through it, and to be breathless with effort does not mean that the effort which produced the breathlessness was thorough or successful.

In two situations especially retrievers reveal their limitations. Heavy bramble often holds rabbits or pheasants, especially hen, which will not flush at the entry of a dog into the clump but have to be systematically hunted out; this operation, routine for a spaniel, is cause for pride when a retriever does it. Where woodland has been thinned or brashed, fallen branches lie for years before rotting down, and tunnels form beneath them where, again, rabbits and pheasants tuck up. Retrievers do not, perhaps cannot because of their size, often work out these tunnels by actually getting into them, which is also basic work for spaniels, especially cockers which have a ferret-like side to their working method.

Retrievers are not to be blamed for their shortcomings in these directions. It would be remarkable if their questing for body scent (i.e., unshot game)

112

was as keen as that of spaniels, which have been bred uninterruptedly to quest for it for many centuries. In their shorter separate history of a century and a half retrievers have been bred the other way, actually to ignore body-scent and to quest only for blood-scent (i.e., that of shot game).

Notwithstanding their lower level of performance in this respect, there are situations in which retrievers have very definite value as hunters-up – because of, not despite, their higher element of serving instinct compared with hunting instinct. The case of gamekeepers is perhaps the most graphic example of those who, actively engaged in sport, may need an all-round gundog with rather less head of steam than that expected in a working spaniel. On a shooting day a keeper has many things on his mind, especially if single-handed. He must keep contact with his employer and the Guns, marshal his beaters, place his stops, control the line during drives, take care of the game, and keep his eyes open for countless local details – all in addition to working his dog. The man who can cope easily with a lively spaniel amid all these distractions is even more rare than the spaniel which does not need coping with. And that, in essence, is what a keeper requires.

A gamekeeper's dog should have the qualities of a huntsman's horse. Both should do their jobs virtually without supervision. A keeper is likely to be at least a competent dog handler, and a huntsman at least a competent horseman. It is not that either of them is unable to control his animal, but that each of them has so much else to do that he is better off if spared the effort. The huntsman's preoccupation is with his hounds; his horse is no more than the vehicle which keeps him near them, and he hopes it will do this with minimum demands on his attention. A gamekeeper wants his dog to put in the air as many as possible of the pheasants which the beaters walk over, and to retrieve any that may be shot by walking Guns – again, with minimum demands on his attention. For his purposes, as for the shooter who feels himself not up to the faster tempo of spaniel work, a retriever of the right type may be the best dog.

Perhaps the ideal is a golden retriever of a particular stamp familiar at shoots. Shorter coated than the show strains, less racy than the field trial specialists, close-coupled and cobby, they use to the full all the virtues of their breed. Such goldens are calm dogs, not give to over-ambition such as trying to quarter half the parish, but ready to stay close if told to, after which they can be left to get on with the job. They are not fast, but plug on steadily at their own pace, dauntless cover penetrators, always sensible, good markers of a falling bird, able to find most of the game that comes down, willing swimmers and with bottomless stamina that outlasts a hard day. To a gundog connoisseur, they are perhaps a little less than thrilling, but thrills are the last things a keeper needs.

I have seen some useful labradors working in the same capacity for keepers, including a brace of bitches which proved on inquiry to have been bred in Warwickshire by Mrs Gwen Broadley, whose Sandylands strain is best known for success in the show ring. Their work was close, thorough, intelligent, and almost wholly self-controlled. They did not, however, cause me to revise my opinion that when it comes to working out really thick stuff when no shot has been fired, a good golden is better than a good labrador, and both are inferior to a springer spaniel which, being smaller and quicker, makes good such cover more thoroughly and in less time.

Several experienced keepers, known to me, work flatcoated retrievers at hunting-up in the beating line. I must declare a personal prejudice in favour of the flatcoat, but cannot believe it ideal in this role. What has been well described as 'the flatcoat's setteryness' makes the close ground treatment which this work requires very difficult to maintain. However, the flatcoat does have a valuable supplementary benefit from this same cause; if allowed to, it will point close-lying unshot birds, and remain staunch on point. This minor skill is especially valuable on cocks-only days, when birds are often found well out on bracken hillsides, or under fallen trees, wide of the nearest Gun. The point provides time for him to get into position to shoot.

There are other instances in which a technical fault in gundog work has its practical uses in the field. Most of them are transmitted along the genetic lines of breed or strain, and therein lies the reason for their being stigmatised officially as faults. If not condemned outright, they may become both exaggerated and ineradicable, so that what would be acceptable in moderation among individuals becomes an unalterable defect when inherent in the whole breed. An example, which I mention with due caution, is giving tongue.

Tongue is very properly regarded as a major fault in any gundog. If recurrent, it soon becomes an intolerable nuisance. Yet I find myself welcoming this trait when a dog tongues on rabbits, provided it does not do so on anything else. Welsh springers often have this happy knack. I am moderate enough as a shot to appreciate prior warning that what is coming will not be airborne, and observation of my companions suggests that I am not alone in this.

Another fault not without value in particular cases concerns flushing. Of course a hunting spaniel should flush its game without hesitation; there can be no argument about that. But for myself there are times when I am thankful for a degree of deliberation. One of our English springers, of happy memory, soon learned this. The sequence of events seemed to graft itself on to my shooting. A sharper, lower tail action would be followed by an accelerating thrust in the hunting; then a pause, tail still going; a raised head, and our eyes would meet across a patch of bramble; hers would flash the questions 'Feet in the right place?' 'Loaded?' 'Thumb on safety catch?'; mine would give her the office 'Push him up!' In she would go; up would go the bird; up, too, went the gun in response to a chain of reflexes which began when her tail first quickened.

Such inter-confidence, team-work and mutual pleasure gives dog-work its special flavour in rough-shooting. Amid the formalities of driven-game the dog is an appendage, performing an ancillary role. In the constantly moving sport of rough-shooting, full of shared endeavours and changing fortunes, the dog is as much a participant as the man. Together, they form a unit. Such a combination transcends 'breed'. Where the trust exists, the ancestry is unimportant, save in the respect that the capacity for trust is best found in dogs whose forebears have been transmitting it over many generations of work to the gun. Subject only to this, all such partnerships begin with personal preference.

Mine is for English springers. Their qualities do not negate those of other breeds, but they are positive, and appeal to me. They combine gentleness with indomitable courage which makes cover and obstacles penetrable, and the joy in life to raise human spirits by their mere presence. In the worst of weather, and in the total absence of game, their willingness does not wane. They are all-rounders, as useful at retrieving as at hunting-up, quick to develop the skills and minor tactics demanded by different types of country. For me they have no superior, but in a certain respect they have an equal. Where cover is most severe is the place for Welsh springers, with their dauntless courage and endless stamina. Where it is softer, especially if also rabbity, the cockers come into their own.

Cover penetration must rank highest in the order of priorities, since the initial questing is more important than the capacity to retrieve. But the margin is not wide in the case of runners. If the game is dead it can eventually be found, if necessary by human persistence alone. But if it is shot but not dead, it must be found as speedily as possible, and in that process only successful dog-work achieves the objective.

Even then, the basic truth remains that unless the game is located and flushed in the first instance, there will be nothing to shoot, so the question of retrieving will not arise. No branch of the sport more clearly establishes the realities. A gundog's purpose is to enable game to be brought to hand; how it does so is a secondary matter. But if the birds are not put into the air, or ground game into the open, this cannot happen. The hunt is the platform on which all other processes, not only in rough-shooting, but all shooting, including that in which the 'hunt' is performed by human beaters, are founded. It is the *raison d'être* in this country of pointer-retrievers which many rough-shooters in open country find attractive and effective. Speaking without experience, I would expect a reduced value from them in woodland. Their pointing can be helpful only where there is inter-visibility between man and dog.

One of the lost pleasures of which the present pattern of shooting, with its emphasis on driven game, has deprived so many of its followers is their own active part in the art of the dog. Many, perhaps most of those who are 'shooting men' today, are precisely that, and no more. They shoot; birds fall; and that, to them, is that. Their contact with what went on before and after the trigger was pulled is minimal, leaving them with a much reduced share of what was formerly the full pleasure.

At a Spaniel Championship my companion for an hour or two was a top-class performer at driven game. After seeing a succession of spaniels which were also top-class performers at their role, he remarked, 'I've shot for thirty-two seasons, and for the first time I'm seeing what spaniel work really is. I suppose it's because I haven't got a gun in my hands.' In reply I cited those who did have guns in their hands, at that time and in that place – the four official Guns who could shoot pheasants cleanly, rabbits equally cleanly (not a universal accomplishment), and read dogs. 'I've been watching them,' my friend answered, 'they gave me the clue. There's more to it than I realised.' His admission did not surprise me.

Those who are orientated on driven game think of a gundog's objective as retrieving, and its function prior to that stage as being to do nothing until told. It being apparent that gundogs also operate with the beaters, they are generally presumed to work as human beaters do, disturbing as much cover as possible, and flushing such birds as are alarmed by this (a decreasing pro-portion as the season advances).

Driven game shooters are concerned with pheasants and partridges when airborne. Unless airborne, the game might as well not be there at all, and how it becomes airborne is outside their purview. Ground, to them, is merely the reception area of the birds when dead. No man's morals or civic worth are any the worse for these beliefs; they arise simply from a frame of mind not easily avoided by those who shoot driven game exclusively. Once, at an estate where I was not a Gun that day, I was asked to reinforce a thinnish beating line by working a brace of spaniels. My place was in the centre, flanked by two walking Guns twenty yards on either side of me, all the human element being deployed outside them on the two flanks. Both were farmers, and excellent shots. Neither, it later transpired, had ever shot over spaniels, which in effect was what they were then called upon to do. We were in forest oaks, much thinned five years back, the ground cover being bramble, some bracken, and occasional rhododendron clumps.

Each carried his gun over his arm, where it remained until a bird was put up, or somebody shouted 'Back!' Each walked a straight course, both had their eyes inclined upwards – towards the air where, in their experience, the birds would be seen. When the time-honoured cry of 'Rabbit back' was raised, there was a hasty change of emphasis and ground level came under inspection for the first time. Another time-honoured cry, 'Damn and blast', no less, fell from the lips of the right-hand walking Gun. A woodcock, pushed out by a spaniel, had done what woodcock can be trusted to do, flushed and gone away on the blind side of a rhododendron clump, denying him a shot. He would have had a shot had he altered course for five or six paces when the dog first feathered. But, eyes in the air, he either did not see this, or did not grasp the significance of what the dog was doing.

By contrast, the Guns at that Championship were not looking in the air. To them the ground was not only the destination for dead birds, but the launching pad for live ones. They were watching the dogs, well knowing that they would receive advance information by so doing. When birds were flushed their guns were no longer over their arms; they were half way to being mounted; their feet, moreover, were clear of undergrowth. Not being taken by surprise, they did not miss much.

Reading the dog, a phase without application at the pegs until the pick-up begins, means more than keeping an eye on an evidently energetic creature which is assumed to be doing purposeful things. It means anticipating correctly the developing situation as revealed by what the dog is doing. This is also the reason for the importance of style in a spaniel. A stylish spaniel's tail action and head carriage indicate to the knowing eye when he has winded game (which he does not find by accident but by nose), how he is progressing towards flushing it, and what the game is likely to be. A momentary doubtful pause can mean woodcock, a confident plunge into covert signals pheasant, and a hectic crackling and upheaval in the depths indicate that a rabbit is being worked. Experience provides many refinements and variations on those themes.

When working together, the Gun and the dog are co-equals. But the dog has the initiative, and a Gun is behind the game (no pun intended) if he fails to take advantage of this. Not to do so is like ignoring the bidding at bridge. To be 'with' a good spaniel in all its actions brings an extra dimension into the sport before a shot is fired, and the only cost is a little extra concentration.

If I were asked to recommend a dog for an owner whose chief interest would be wildfowling, I would regard the request as an extreme instance of a familiar problem. The 'breed' is valuable as a preliminary guide. What decides the eventual choice for any function is whether a particular owner likes a particular dog, and whether the dog likes him. Even if the dog does not belong to a breed evolved for whatever is in mind, where this bond exists the dog in question is probably the best choice, provided it is not going to be asked to do the impossible.

The impossible, for a gundog with a sincere desire to please its master (which in effect is what 'well-bred' means in this context) is an ever-receding term. Dogs thus motivated are capable of performances which by all the rules of reason ought to be beyond them. Nevertheless there are limits which commonsense and consideration require to be applied.

In this specific case, wildfowling belongs to a rugged world. Mud is deep and clinging; gutters steep-sided and slippery; down them the tide races, bearing shot birds towards the sea; the wind is always cold to a dog which in that setting cannot hope to be dry, and sometimes it is freezing; there are days when a dog's only hope of warmth is when it is swimming – and that, of course, is inevitably followed by a further spell of frost-exposure. It is hardly an environment into which to take a cocker spaniel, although I shall not be surprised when somebody tells me of a cocker which performs magnificently at wildfowling and thoroughly enjoys doing so. There is always an exception and this of all breeds can rise above (and sink below) the limits applicable to most others. But if not a cocker spaniel, then what?

Obviously, I would expect to find an ideal water-worker and weather-resister most easily from a stoutly-bred line of labradors. As a breed, they are the best swimmers of all. Even when the swimming they do is within the compass of other breeds, this still has a plus value; having swum, their energies and stamina are less depleted for whatever other missions and endurance await them. But the prospective owner may not particularly like labradors, there being no accounting for the vagaries of human preference. In that case, English springers of some strains are nearly their equal. These are not, of course, of the light, quick-moving kind which are ever more popular for inland game-shooting. They are the robust, heavier coated, square-rigged type, often bred especially for this very job. The critical factor in a spaniel is that it should be up to the weather as well as up to the work.

Every wildfowler hopes to shoot a goose. If he does, the dog is not yet bred which will not be severely tested in retrieving it. Merely bringing it in across mudflats calls for great strength properly co-ordinated, and this is the least of the likely problems. Swimming with it against a current in tidal channels or sluices, carrying it into, across and out of gutters calls for a relatively herculean performance guided by initiative and determination which must not be undermined by exhaustion.

Wildfowling is not for weaklings or valiant lightweights. Whatever their qualities, such dogs should not be asked to do it. There are other possibilities. Flatcoated retrievers, excelled only by labradors as water dogs, and their equal in love of it, often take to wildfowling exceptionally well. Golden retrievers are as capable of it. Traditionally, wildfowling is the natural work of curly-coated retrievers and Irish water spaniels. The oil rather than the curl in the coats of each gives them a margin in weather resistance denied to others. In its country of origin, the latter is regarded as a retriever rather than a spaniel, and in wildfowling conditions its tendency to self-determination is an advantage rather than the embarrassment it can be elsewhere.

Given that a good gundog can be of any breed, but that the physical requirements are most likely to be found in the six now named, the other qualities which constitute a good wildfowler's dog must be considered. High among them is the difficult requirement that it must be as near invisible as possible. This is partly a matter of colour camouflage, partly of keeping still. Retriever breeds are self-coloured. Perhaps those which are not black have the best chance of merging into the landscape, but this advantage is slight. Spaniels are broken-coloured, liver or black and white, this being a recognised advantage in camouflage. This advantage, too, is slight and certainly less important than immobility.

If his master is to have some shooting on foreshore or saltings, it is imperative that the dog should keep still. Freedom from fidgeting will not be achieved unless there is total confidence and unity of purpose between the two. Hence the paramount need that they should be, in the sporting sense, in love with each other, and the transcendent importance of the individual over the breed. Fidgeting, like whining, is a consequence of discontent and in wildfowling this is most likely to arise from hardship of the surroundings and the weather. To be insistent on the dog's capacity to endure both without stress is therefore no mere humanitarian fad. It is prerequisite to the attainment of the objective.

The seemingly simple matter of retrieving from or across water illustrates the differences of method between the three groups of gundog breeds to whose lot this work naturally falls (the pure pointing breeds being of course excluded). One afternoon in spring demonstrated the contrasts not merely

119

for me, but for a large galley of spectators. It happened that I was judge of the water section of one of the Game Conservancy National Retrieving Test area semi-finals, which was held at the Conservancy's headquarters at Burgate Manor, which stand above a loop of the Hampshire Avon at Fordingbridge. At one stage the dogs were required to pick dummies which had fallen into the river, in sight of them and saluted by gunshot.

As usual, this was more difficult on the day than the verbal description suggests, and certainly more difficult than retrieving across the river, as distinct from out of it, would have been. All but one of the twenty-two competitors accomplished it, a fact indicative of the quality of the dogs, not of an undemanding problem. The Avon had been a big river all spring, and heavy water was coming down. The main flow was under the far bank, which was where the dummy fell. There the current swung strongly on the arc of a convex curve, accelerating to a point fifty yards downstream, where it began to race. Between the dogs' departure point and the line along which the dummies were carried, lay twenty-five yards or so of dead water.

This was therefore no simple matter of dogs marking the fall, swimming out, and picking the dummy. The collection had to be made before the dummy reached the point where the race began. At dog's eye-level, keeping it in view in popply water cannot have been easy, perhaps not always possible. Success therefore depended on an accurate estimate by the dog of its own speed through water which was first sluggish then fast moving, and of the speed of the dummy so that its future position could be gauged accurately enough for the dog to make the rendezvous in time. Similar problems are familiar to such persons as the captains of warships and, in my own less sophisticated experience, to anti-tank gunners. We had such aids as range-finders, predictors and deflection sights, but in the heat of the moment depended on our common sense; which of course, was what the dogs did. But how? Their procedures were interesting.

My practice as judge was to hold each dog for a count of five after the dummy had splashed, to establish steadiness, then to send the dog. No dog failed to mark. That was where overall similarity ended.

Every labrador launched itself, not directly towards the dummy, but on a course laid-off about fifteen per cent downstream. All of them made their interception without having to correct their line by more than a foot or two in the last few yards. Their estimate of their own pace, and that of the dummy, and their capacity to relate the two, was almost flawlessly accurate. Labradors, with their powerful swim, leave an appreciable wake. For me, standing directly behind them as they crossed the dead water, it was easy to follow the line they had taken. In every case this was straight, not curved as

120

it would have been had a dog been bending its own course towards a visibly moving target.

English springer spaniels were equally unanimous on a different plan. Their downstream lay-off of course was much greater, about thirty per cent. Having reached the fast water under the far bank they then turned upstream, stemming the tide so to speak, and trod water until the dummy was swept down to them. This gave them the advantage of a lessened contest with the cross-current on the outward swim, but the disadvantage of having to start their return swim from a point further downstream than the labradors did. A canine opinion on which was the better plan was provided by the representatives of two minority breeds. It was, however, a split verdict.

A competent Irish water spaniel took the more direct course of the labrador, making contact with the same precision. The profuse coat of this breed, acting like a buoyancy belt, makes the swimming style also similar to the labrador, shoulders prominently above the waterline. Golden retrievers did it the spaniel way. In the conditions this exercise was sufficiently severe to test not only the dogs' willingness to swim, but their standard of performance too. In heavy water the dog which seems determined to punch a hole through the current saves distance and therefore time (a practical consideration when a Gun has two or more duck down, and more flighting in). No dog in this state allowed the dummy to get downstream of him. Had this happened a dog would have been in great difficulty if the dummy had reached the 'race'. Those entered were, by virtue of the qualifications, relatively experienced and most had much shooting behind them.

These distinctive styles in performing fundamentally identical operations are of practical significance to a trainer in the process of bringing out the best in his dogs. They tell him what to expect. But to put both them and the training process into perspective it is necessary to remind oneself of the real priorities of gundog work, and how that work fits into the present-day shooting scene. Sometimes the expressions used by sporting people, as a kind of verbal shorthand, distort what is actually the case, or imply a meaning which has become outmoded.

No better compliment can be paid to a gundog than saying that it 'puts game in the bag'. This, indeed, is the end-product of all gundog endeavours, even for pointers and setters which in Britain seldom take any part in the proceedings after the shot is fired, and hence have no actual contact with the game. It is the physical acts most immediately leading up to putting game in the bag – the pick-up and the carry-back – which express to all beholders, spectators no less than the satisfied owner, success in the mission and remain predominant in their consciousness.

But the actions which compose this triumphant finale do not constitute the mission itself, and are in fact only the tip of the iceberg. An almost totally useless dog can pick up and carry back game which has fallen on stubble or plough forty yards or so from the peg. Thereby it saves its Gun some effort in walking and stooping, which is doubtless welcome, but hardly world-shattering. The real work of retriever, spaniel, or any other dog serving the gun is not in fetching and carrying, but in finding what is to be fetched and carried. As stated, all game has to be found twice, before it is shot and afterwards. Both phases contribute equally to putting game in the bag under the traditional conditions of rough-shooting, and both are performed by spaniels, retrievers acting as spaniels, and by pointer-retrievers. In driven-game shooting, however, the 'before' stage is generally carried out by beaters, perhaps helped by spaniels, and the 'afterwards' by pickers-up, except for the game falling dead within sight of the Guns.

The two operations have thus become distinct from each other; distinct, too, from that of the dogs which sit in the line as their masters shoot, and retrieve only in the 'afterwards' phase. This separation of roles, as old as the breech-loading gun but much magnified recently, leads back to the question, 'Which is the ideal breed for picking up?' It is a very important question, since the great majority of finds which cannot be made without a capable dog are nowadays made by the pickers-up and not by the Guns themselves.

No answer can be attempted without recognising what 'picking-up' amounts to. The term misleads, being over-simple. It suggests the process which is in fact carried out by the Guns' dogs, the gathering of the game which has fallen round the pegs. But what it actually means is the pursuit, location and recovery of birds which flew on having been hit, and came down in places too distant to be precisely known. Hunting-up would be a better term than picking-up.

Those who are present at a shoot to work dogs in this capacity operate in scales of time and distance very different from those applying to dogs worked by the Guns or in the beating line. Whatever the Guns' dogs do must be accomplished before the Land Rovers leave for the next stand, the beaters and their dogs having already left. The pickers-up are under no such constraint – or if they are, they should not be. If he takes an hour to find a single bird, a picker-up is doing his job. If he picks six in three minutes he is doing what somebody else could do equally well. He is not there to 'pick' the easy birds, but to seek out and bring back the difficult ones. Those which fall within gunshot, if dead, will not move. It is not beyond the wit and resource of man to gather them unaided. Those which are hit but do not fall forthwith are another matter.

The shot pheasant which glides on and comes down in kale half a mile away, arousing the comment 'That'll be a dead bird' from those who do not have to go for it, is clearly one for a picker-up. So are all the others which, saluted by calls of 'Mark that one', still fly on until they slant down behind shelter belts or into bracken patches, or are lost to sight as they swerve into a wood. Pickers-up have far to go in pursuit of them, and many possibilities to take into account, not excluding the coefficient of inherent veracity of the Gun who bore witness.

Time was when I considered retrievers ideal collaborators in such operations. When well trained they can be worked at greater distance than most spaniels, if only because normal spaniel work gives fewer chances to develop really remote control. This, it seemed, should reduce the handler's leg-work. Experience has made me less sure of the value of this reduction. Unless the fall of a bird is accurately known, and a dog can be brought to it promptly, its probable whereabouts can only be conjectured. The search for it then becomes a process of elimination. Likely areas of ground are searched systematically, and to know where the bird is not becomes in many cases an essential preliminary to arriving at where it is. At this stage saving one's legs is a minor consideration beside that of being sure that ground has been thoroughly hunted.

It is unreasonable to expect a retriever to hunt a forty-yard beat, say of brambles, as systematically as a spaniel, though it may be the equal of any spaniel at cover-penetration when on a line, or when going for a marked retrieve. That simply is not a retriever's trade. But it is what a spaniel lives for. Figures of speech can reveal unconscious truth, and the idiom of the human partners is of more than philological interest. Often I have noticed that a keeper with a retriever at heel will say as he passes after a drive, 'Just run your dog through this bit; there may be something in it.' Those with spaniels put it otherwise. 'Try hunting this piece out' is their expression. And there is a difference.

No skin off either nose, but the old tag about owners and dogs applies. When a spaniel has 'hunted' his ground and drawn a blank, I know there is nothing there, and that the time has come to try somewhere else. When a retriever has 'run through' it, I am less sure. When all is quiet, I sometimes put a spaniel in behind him, not always without something to show for it.

Without doubt, the general level of spaniel and retriever work has been greatly raised in the five completed post-war decades. Regular observation at shoots is enough to convince anybody of this who has a memory long enough to make a comparison. The reasons lie partly in the improving quality and trainability of the best working strains – a kind of man-assisted evolution; partly in the emergence of picking-up almost as a separate sport in its own right, where handlers with no other interest set themselves standards beyond the reach of those to whom dog-work is secondary to the shooting; partly in the example set by field trials in showing what is possible at the sharp end of competition; and partly in better methods of training developed (and readily shared) by the best professionals.

Improvement is less marked in the pointing breeds. The decline of partridge shooting because of farming changes, and the extension of driving on most grouse moors to the exclusion of shooting over dogs, has led to the disbanding of most kennels of these dogs maintained by great estates, and the consequent loss of professional handlers. Their competent, sporting, and increasingly numerous amateur successors are thus denied the pace-setters of the past. Nevertheless, this attractive form of dog-work offers great opportunities to those good enough to take them, and its great days may yet be restored. Any endeavour pursued with determination and intelligence over a period leads to general improvement.

If the further factor of purposeful genetic selection is added, improvement becomes marked in any kind of livestock. Hens lay more eggs, cows give more milk, pigs gain more weight, all in a few generations. For gundogs these considerations apply doubly. There is a human factor as well as a canine factor, and the question is often raised as to whether either or both these factors have deteriorated.

My belief that they have improved is not based on opinions, whether of those with long memories or of past writers. Old men forget, and for all of us the past glows more rosily than the future which we shall not see. Better to rely on the facts of life. Evolution, the process which perfects every life-form in relation to its life-style, is perpetual and, left to itself, prevents deterioration. Breeding – improving on natural selection because it removes the elements of chance and distance and is orientated to a specific purpose – greatly accelerates the evolutionary process. Hence it is more likely than not that the gundogs of today are better than those of yesteryear.

Whether the trainers and handlers are better is an issue clouded by sentiment. Just as the canonisation of saints is delayed by many generations in order that the cool verdict of history may supplant warmly biased living opinion, so the giants of living memory retain their stature and seem irreplaceable while that memory lasts. Beyond doubt the 'greats' of the immediate post-war scene were superb. Nobody would be big-headed enough to claim to stand on a level with such great professionals as Kent, Greatorex, Hill, Forbes, Abbott, Manners, and Male (to spare the blushes of those old-timers still competing), or with such gifted amateurs as Major

H. M. Peacock, Mason Prime or Hal Jackson, until the logic of results put them there. But what is forgotten is that these men were pioneers. They took up the art when gundog training came out of its dark ages. What they discovered, formulated and passed on has been handed down and spread around by example and word of mouth, distilled into books, and is freely applied by the trainers of today, professional or amateur. Thanks to them, our raw material is better than theirs. The effect of the old masters on the sporting gundogs of present and future is not lessened by the fact of their having left the scene, but a gain because they were for so long part of it.

The conclusion is that spaniels today are, in general level, better and more trainable than those of the past, this being repeatedly remarked. Their trainers operate with the advantage of knowledge accumulated and codified only in the first half of the twentieth century, and not available to those of the more distant past. It would be curious, these things being so, if present standards were worse, or if future standards became worse, than those of their predecessors. My own small experience confirms this. Only a decade ago style and polish in the retrieve at spaniel trials was regarded off-handedly by most handlers and by at least half the judges. So long as the game came back unharmed few cared about the transit process. Now polish in the pick-up, carry and delivery are as important as in retriever trials. A spaniel handler asked to 'handle out' more than thirty-five yards in those days professed martyrdom. Not so now. Retrieving range in spaniel trials comes near to having doubled.

A chance remark by an elderly acquaintance supported my impression. 'In my day,' he said (referring to field trials thirty years earlier) 'if you had a steady dog you'd be in the first four.' There are no soft field trials any more. Very few sub-standard dogs run in public. The winner at any level must visibly excel every one of his rivals, since fewer and fewer defeat themselves; and competition is tough, very tough, at the top.

Competition, of course, is not typical. It is the small peak of the large pyramid of practical working dogs. But it is also the proving ground of the blood-lines from which nearly all the workers came, and hence operates as two sorts of guide. It indicates where the best material is, and it provides evidence as to where the richest seams of gundog birthright have become concentrated.

I believe that we who train gundogs at this time are very fortunate in the material which we can use, and that in time to come our successors will think back to the millennium as a golden age. Its records speak for themselves; all it lacks, for us who are part of it, is glamour. For the reasons stated, glamour is visible only in the long view back.

What moderns inevitably lack, *vis-à-vis* the figures of the past, is the lustre which grows round names famed over many years not only in action but in printed records. To compare present with past we must compare what we have observed with what we have come to imagine on the strength of earlier people's opinions. My own present opinion (which will one day become of the past) is that modern professionals are not so humdrum as to have let things slide, that the dogs of today are as good as the evidence suggests, and that as the years pass such names as the Chudleys, the Wylies, MacKenzie, Meldrum, Bremner, White-Robinson, Erlandson, Macqueen, and the Openshaw generation will stand beside the great men of the history of which they will then have become part.

10

THE PARADOX OF SPEED

Earlier the point was made that every gundog virtue has its compensating vice, and most gundog qualities are faults in reverse. It is the trainer's aim to direct each dog's private inborn ambitions, never better described than in the words of Prayer Book as the devices and desires of its own heart, towards useful employment in aid of the shooter. This is especially true of speed, a great blessing in a good dog and the root of most evil in a bad one.

One of the greatest of trainers, John Kent, said this of speed in relation to young dogs in the development stage, 'Once we know they *can* go fast, we spend the next twelve months trying to slow them down.' I cannot remember any other eighteen words which have expressed for me so much that is essential to the training process. To gain their inner meaning it is first necessary to appreciate that in this sense there are two applications of the concept of speed.

Speed may mean the pace at which a dog works effectively, or it may mean mere velocity. The former is highly desirable, adding to the effectiveness and thrill of the dog's performance; the latter, misdirected, as an unmitigated curse, multiplying whatever failings a dog may have and transforming into a positive menace an animal which would otherwise be no worse than negatively useless. Think therefore of pace – pace of work, pace of reflex and response, quickness in the uptake as situations develop – as the practical concept of speed in a gundog.

For pointers and setters pace, properly applied, enables wider beats to be covered without slowing-down the Guns. Unless speed is used laterally, pushing out to the flanks, its sole consequence is the useless one of covering a narrower beat more rapidly – and causing the Guns to waste breath in hurrying to keep up.

In retrievers pace is valuable in getting a dog quickly to a marked fall. A winged bird may immediately begin running strongly, almost as fast as it had been flying, so every split second is vital in enabling the dog to get on to the line at its freshest, thereby gaining the confidence to work it out immediately and wholeheartedly. Pace in a retriever also helps in hunting out doubtful ground, provided it is not achieved in exchange for thoroughness, and adds its hallmark of style and efficiency in achieving a prompt return.

Spaniels, in doing the most varied and the most basic of gundog work, give a close-up view of the value of well-used pace. Not only does it enhance the pleasure of dog-work properly done in the eyes of discriminating sportsmen, but it has great operational advantages. The shock effect of a fast dog penetrating cover gets things happening. A clapped pheasant or a seated rabbit, initially determined to 'stay put' unless directly pushed out, is likely to lose its nerve and move, thereby disclosing its presence when a brisk, brave and businesslike spaniel turns its attention to a clump of cover, treating it as a commando soldier would. A turn of foot, and the confidence to use it, also saves pointer-retrievers from the cardinal sin of keeping the Guns waiting. But what is common to all gundogs is not to be used in identical ways by all of them. Each individual dog must come to terms with the fact of its own pace, and learn to turn it on when desirable, turn if off again when not, and always to relate it to the conditions of the ground and the day.

In all essential respects the use of pace by a gundog is a constructive contradiction identical with that of speed in a hunter when ridden to hounds. A wise foxhunter once said, expatiating on the advantages of a thoroughbred horse in the hunting field: 'The thing is, if he can gallop he'll never need to.' He meant that such a horse's canter would be good enough, so that while lesser animals were at full stretch, the thoroughbred would still be going easily. This is precisely why pace is valuable in a gundog. The top speed of a fast dog will seldom or never be needed. But it enables the dog to go at its own half speed and still be faster than others – in other words, to work quickly without hurrying.

The difference between gundog and horse is that a rider can control the speed of his horse, but a gundog must do its own controlling. To show it the need to do so, without knocking the edge of its physical pace and mental initiative, is one of the finer points of training. For speed in all its applications, good and bad, even the lack of it, is something to be coped with in every dog.

The young of every species fall in love with speed. All good retrievers and spaniels, if they are worth their salt, go through this phase. Springer spaniels are perhaps the nearest in approach to the human ton-up boy, glorying in covering the ground and the excitement of making fast turns. All the retrievers, especially flatcoats with their setter blood, run them close. Cocker spaniels, always quick to learn from experience anything which acts to their own advantage, are probably the first to learn to adapt their tempo to the limitations imposed by the cover in which they are working and by what their noses are telling them.

Generally it is near the end of its first full season that a retriever or spaniel of other breeds appreciates that discretion adds to the rewards of enthusiasm. The fact suddenly dawns that scent varies and so does cover, and that more game is found with less delay if pace is regulated accordingly. Experience alone can teach this. The trainer's role is limited to the careful introduction of increasingly difficult situations, never over-facing the dog, always encouraging it to use its own judgement. The bad-scenting day when a dog goes out to a mark like a greyhound from the slips and, having reached it, changes down two gears and 'plaits' the surrounding area, is a red-letter one to the man in charge. A very important penny will have dropped.

The questing breeds are not directly comparable. They work more remote from their handlers, so can be less directly helped. Normally they have only two paces – top speed and stop. Their dominant inborn wish is to keep moving at top pitch, whether it is the ground-eating, long-striding canter of the pointers, the tireless airy grace of Irish setters, or the concentrated, purposeful, unrelenting gallop of English or Gordon setters. Only slowly are the problems realised – the day of sunburned heather which holds little scent, or the windless day when the sticky air is trickling down the moorland slopes, filling and spilling from the hollows at unexpected angles. Then the careful dog which drops his pace yet keeps his awareness at full alert can be admired for his skill in stopping promptly enough to avoid running into his birds. He will probably be a five-year-old or more.

Speed in an animal, as in Man, is not solely dependent on physique (which is another instance in which breed standards are false presumptions as means of assessment). Without efficient conformation, speed is impossible or short-lived. But efficient conformation alone does not produce it. The governing factor is nerve transmission, the synchronising and accelerating of the neuro-electrical impulses which motivate and co-ordinate the muscles. From this comes leg-speed in the human athlete, class in the racehorse, and style in the gundog. In this connection the mere fact of speed, as distinct from the uses to which it is put, can be a revealing indicator of the quality of a dog's nervous efficiency.

The co-ordination which makes speed possible does not stop at that. A nervous system is indivisible. The capacity for slick response to stimulus which produces swift smooth movement when the brain demands it will be equally prompt and accurate in producing other responses, too. Tail action – vigorous, positive and in rhythm with leg action – is another example. A quick dog is likely to be a keen dog, the kind of dog which turns on a sixpence at a single whistle pip. And a dog which reacts instantly to a single whistle pip will do likewise to a single touch of scent, making something of a clue which a more solid dog might fail to exploit.

This is not to say that a more stolid dog would not have its uses. Men and women vary as much as dogs do. Not all are built for speed. Not all are quick reactors, and there is no universal wish to be. Everybody's ideal dog for shooting over, or for picking-up, differs in some way from everybody else's, and for this reason every form of guide, however small, is helpful in assessing the characteristics, temperament, and approach to life of every gundog-to-be so that it could be moulded in training to meet the needs of its eventual possessor. It is no sin to have preferences and, since the only real measure of a gundog's worth is the extent to which it meets the need of its human partner, there is as much room for the patent-safety type as for field trial fliers. What is important is that neither category should be stupid.

One of the consequences of the domination of British spaniel work by springers is that the field of choice is thereby limited, particularly in the matter of speed. Being as unchallenged in the competitive field as the thoroughbred horse is in racing, the whole breed has tended to become faster. This is much to the liking of those with the footwork, concentration, and general activity to match. But for others the wish is for a dog which does its job in a more deliberate way. For them the mercurial cocker manner is not always the answer, which is more likely to lie in the minority spaniel breeds. One reason for the probability is that a springer which does not move as fast as is normal for the breed may owe its comfortable cadence to the fact that it cannot think fast. In their present state of development minority breed spaniels do not move fast, however quickly they think.

The term minority breeds is nowadays taken to mean all spaniels other than English and Welsh springer and cocker. Of those which remain, the Irish water spaniel's prime use is as a retriever (it is classified as such in its country of origin). The others are the Clumber, the Sussex and the field (the last breed, together with occasional cockers, to be run in trials against English springers). The problem in all of them is to identify and re-fortify the working strains.

In recent seasons I have seen Clumbers and Sussex, and one smartly impressive field spaniel, in action at shoots. They demonstrated that they could do their jobs, albeit with something less than the dispatch which is expected of springers. But to expect either to perform at English springer pace would be as unreasonable as expecting amply built members of the Pioneer Corps to keep in step with Light Infantry. They are just not made that way. Nor, of course, are shooting men all made the same way; and they are not all the same age. Some may be better able, and more willing, to keep in step with a Clumber rather than with a springer. Moreover the emergence of dog-work as a second echelon in the sport of shooting, separate from though in support of the use of the gun, has produced a specialised corps of well-skilled dog-handlers – men and women of many different backgrounds finding in this a satisfying way to enjoy the trinity of game and gun and dog and well able to get the best out of whichever breed best suits them. This confirms that it is no longer sensible, if indeed it ever was, to consider the advantages and otherwise of particular breeds of gundog without considering also the characteristics and needs of those who work with them.

11

WORKINGS OF MEMORY

The mental element with which we are most concerned in training and working a gundog is memory. We feed into the dog's memory adjustments to its inborn urges, new skills and responses to particular situations. We hope for rapid, accurate retrieval of what we have put in when the need for it arises; accurate in the sense that the action which the memory stimulates will be one which is actually required. So when we begin training a new puppy we are in effect loading its memory with the things it needs to know. The efficiency with which memory provides the right answers to the endless questions which a gundog encounters throughout its working life will depend on the tidiness and clarity with which we have introduced this information during training. So it is helpful to study the depth and scope of the canine memory in general, and the gundog memory specifically, noting how much it can absorb, and the processes by which a dog uses what it remembers.

Animal memory is non-selective and unadjustable. It takes in the wrong impressions as readily as the right ones (from the human viewpoint). If, inadvertently, we give a puppy a wrong impression – and at times we all do – we cannot say, 'Forget what I've just said' or 'Perhaps it will help if I rephrase that.' Similarly we cannot prevent a puppy forming the wrong association of ideas, except by minimising its opportunities for doing so.

For instance I, like other gundog owners, follow a particular drill at feeding time, not only to maintain good order and discipline, but as an exercise in self-control for the dogs at an occasion which is for them one of high excitability. My practice is to put the feed bowls on the ground, well apart, before opening the kennel doors. The dogs, of course, come bounding out and the meeting is called to order by the command to drop, in one or other of its forms – a raised hand, the word 'hup', or a whistle signal – before they are directed each to its own ration. Even so simple a formality produces a useful experience of misunderstanding, as when one puppy associated the raised hand with the subject then uppermost in its mind, food. For several weeks it anticipated that it was about to be fed whenever the drop was ordered in this form, no matter where or at what time of day.

The high level of gundog intelligence is generally some insurance against confusion of input by the memory. Most of those with working pedigrees, hence descended from ancestors accustomed to using their brains, draw the right conclusions from the fortuitous experiences that come their way. In this they are in contrast with horses, few of which have any ability to use their brains at all, unless to their own direct advantage. For a whole year I had to sit tight on a young mare which always fly-jumped at a certain tree because a small boy had fallen out of it one day as we passed. She never fly-jumped at the tree if my wife was riding her, evidently holding me personally responsible for the dramatic ejection of the small boy, and suspecting that I might repeat the performance. A gundog of average intelligence would never be victim of such a confusion of memories.

The canine mind does have some capability to keep things in proportion. It behoves us to do the same. If, for example, we over-react, and consequently over-correct a dog, at some piece of indiscipline which circumstances (or our own mood) have exaggerated, we may make an undesirably deep impression on a dog's memory. A simple case is that of a dog which, ordered 'stay', crosses a lane down which a car is approaching and narrowly escapes being run over. In the stress of the moment a handler, dealing with the dog's offence in breaking 'stay', may act much more emphatically than the situation – as the dog sees it – justifies and leave an aftermath of confusion, bewilderment, doubt, even fear. But fear of the human in charge, not of the passing car. A dog, having no imagination, cannot consider what might have happened. The trainer must as usual bear the whole responsibility, including that of remembering that in etching the lessons of life on the sensitive surface of memory, equability is the first essential. Without it, firmness may be misleading.

The capacity of dogs' memories varies in potential and develops at differing rates, but most of them have mental blocks on more or less the same subjects. Some dogs can temporarily record multiple memories, others cannot. When a number of birds have fallen in sight of a dog, it is interesting to see how many the dog can retrieve without being given directions; in other words, how many 'marks it can hold'. One of our English springer spaniels could be relied upon to hold five, going straight to each fall successively without further command. If more than five were down it was evident that she could recall the locations of two or three more on being reminded. This was a skill which has faded in gameshooting as the years passed, and she has become increasingly impatient when sitting at stands. But when flighting duck or pigeons, when the volume of shooting and the fall of birds are both less, her mark-memory is as good as ever. I do not recall any of our retrievers holding more marks than this, though one would expect retrievers to be better than spaniels at this particular skill. However well-mannered they may be, few spaniels are naturally happy when sitting at a drive; their hearts are in cover, flushing the birds.

One of the chief mental blocks for a developing dog is judgement of distance. Most retrieving dogs can mark accurately for line almost from the onset of training; estimate of the range from them to their retrieves takes longer to perfect. Almost invariably it is over-estimated. Young dogs often go out eighty yards, over-running their target after thirty yards. For some reason awareness of bearing seems to be in-born; awareness of distance has to be learned. But not from the trainer, for there is no way of teaching it. Experience is the only demonstrator, and the skill comes rapidly when a young dog graduates from dummy work, to which few give their whole souls, to the greater magnetism of working on game.

Another blank in the canine memory mechanism is the time factor. Dogs show no awareness of the passage of time, no means of relating it to the other aspects of their lives. Realisation of this would greatly ease the anxieties of those who must leave their dogs in boarding kennels, and help in devising a sensible close-season regime for working gundogs.

When left in kennels a dog is not conscious of an accumulation of days without seeing its well-loved master. Greatly though it appreciates his eventual appearance, it has not felt mounting resentment at his non-appearance meanwhile. With good food, comfort, cleanliness and the security given by capable attendants, the only stress a dog feels is the initial separation. The way to increase this is to visit the dog, because each visit means another separation. Spared the disappointment of abandonment after each short-lived joy of reunion, a dog can live contentedly. The same is true of gundogs in the close season. They do not deteriorate because they are out of action, provided their health, physical and mental, is successfully maintained. Indeed many gundogs are improved very positively by substantial spells in kennel, particularly between their second and third shooting seasons. The explanation may be that, deprived of action, their memories have been at work. Without the power to imagine, and hence to anticipate the future, their minds have no recourse except to re-live the past. Remembering, perhaps repeatedly, their experiences may explain the new maturity with which dogs perform after a summer's rest. Very often they return not with the boisterousness of unexpended energy, but with a sense of timely purpose notably increased since the end of the preceding season.

This suggests that dogs are less susceptible to boredom than we are, that they have an enviable facility for switching off and being content while inactive. But if they are proof against ennui when doing nothing, they are certainly not proof against that form of boredom which results from excessive interference when working – and this in a manner which involves the memory, and especially the uncanny awareness of one place which has already been mentioned. Place, indeed, is one of the central struts of the canine memory. It is place, exact place preferably to the precise square foot of ground, which re-activates a dog's memory of some episode which constituted misdemeanour, and permits it to be corrected in the certainty that the dog will know the reason for the correction. A dog sent off on a long, exciting hunt for a runner, perhaps collecting it half-a-mile away after long and tortuous working out of the line, is never in any doubt about the place where he left his handler, and returns confidently to it. For the handler to have moved is greatly to reduce the dog's confidence in him. A man or woman who, in the dog's opinion, is unreliable over place cannot thereafter be wholly trusted by the dog.

The process of teaching a dog to work its ground thoroughly, more important to spaniels than to others, often leaves the trainer much wiser, as well as the dog. Essentially, this is something that only the dog can teach itself, by being given the ground and the opportunity, and then left to get on with it under supervision. But trainers can and do help by a measure of insistence that no individual patch of potentially holding cover is left uninvestigated, and herein lies a snag. The dog's own memory for the individual patches is so retentive that it much dislikes being sent back to ground which it has already hunted. Care must be taken that this does not happen inadvertently, because it is as fruitful a cause as any of a dog first resenting, and then ignoring hand and whistle signals.

The conclusion is that though dogs are little liable to become bored when doing nothing, they are very liable to become bored by interruption when they are doing something, whether in action or in training. The deciding opinion of what is excessive is theirs, not ours. In this connection I have read in two standard text books on gundog training, one ancient, one modern, a highly suspect statement on teaching response to hand signals. Each writer used the same unfortunate phrase. 'Constant repetition' of the lesson in question, each declared (more than half a century apart), would make it second nature. Though not untrue, this way of putting it is so misleading that I wonder how both could have succeeded in giving an impression which I am sure neither intended. Perhaps the earlier author chose his words without due thought, and the more recent one subconsciously copied him.

There are two stages in imbuing a dog with every one of its separate skills and disciplines. First the dog must get the message as to what it is required to do, or not do. Secondly, that message must be bedded-in, so that it does indeed become as nearly as possible second nature. The present point is how to achieve this second stage. Basically, the advice quoted is sound. But the terms in which it is conveyed contain the seeds of trouble.

Consider what the quoted words mean. 'Repetition' must be taken to mean giving the lesson again and again, which may well be necessary. But the addition of 'constant' to the repetition adds the qualities of 'continually (viz. without interval)' and 'unchangeably'. This seems to me an effective formula for boring the animal, if not to death then certainly to a degree of non-enthusiasm which may affect its entire working life. Having made this error myself, and thereby spoiled a potentially good retriever, I have a small claim to knowing what I am talking about. More important, fundamentals of animal training in general and gundog training in particular lie contrary to such a course.

If the aim is simply to instil obedience, it may well be that constant repetition is a way to do it, though it would not do for me. But by the time a gundog has reached the stage of hand signals, the objectives of its training are much wider than mere obedience. It is required to use its own initiative in co-operation with its handler, and to choose between options in other situations where its handler cannot help. Anything which restricts this initiative is counter-productive. On the limited issue of hand signals in game (or dummy) finding, the 'bedding-in' process is quite definitely not helped and may actually be hindered by constant repetition. The effective method is by the discreet fabrication of varied situations in which compliance with hand signals leads to the desired result, ensuring that such exercises are not so frequent that they become a bore or, in Army terminology, a 'fatigue'.

The military analogy can be carried further to make a distinction between drill and training. Drill makes certain responses to certain commands second nature to soldiers by constant repetition. As such it is very useful in certain circumstances, such as getting a battalion to Horse Guards Parade and back for Trooping the Colour. But the same men cannot be made effective in active service except by the vastly wider concept which is training. Gundogs obviously need training rather than drilling, in a ratio not less than three to one. The crucial question is how far the idea of 'practice' is applicable to training (as distinct, of course, from drilling). Up to a point, I believe the more intelligent the animal, the less drilling it can take before the quality of the performances begins to deteriorate.

A dog, and especially a working bred gundog, ranks very high in the level of animal intelligence. My belief is that practice is generally unnecessary to it in the sense of maintaining the perfection of specific actions. If a dog has retrieved twenty pheasants properly it will not greatly improve its style and speed by retrieving another two hundred. It will probably retrieve that number anyway in the course of a season, and there is no need to fabricate occasions on which it can do even more retrieving as practice. On the other hand the act of retrieving, by being a service rendered to the handler, may be of great value, not for itself, but in maintaining the man–dog relationship in a state of due discipline. In this case the trainer must not lose sight of what the objective is, and he must be careful not to overdo it, for if he does, the retrieving itself will suffer. It is essential that its repetition should be interesting as well as meaningful, and that it should never be 'constant', so that the dog's freshness and zest does not lose its edge.

Animal intelligence, being much less than human intelligence, has a saving grace. They forget less readily than we do. The various responses of a gundog therefore do not need more than very occasional purposeful practice (say, in preparation for a new season). They will come as readily as when last performed, even after an interval of months, provided the handler has not fallen in the dog's estimation meanwhile, and provided the communication system has not deteriorated through laxity, or the confused use of commands. Drill must not be allowed wholly to lapse, but training is more likely to suffer from being overdone than underdone.

Nevertheless the capacity to absorb training is of course fundamental to a good gundog, while the capacity to learn for itself is essential to make a good one into a better one. Though complementary, the two aptitudes are distinct, and must develop separately. Game sense, which equates to operationally applied memory, is the part that gundogs can learn from their own experience alone, for obviously it cannot be taught to them. We and they operate in different spheres. We view the scene from a relatively elevated standpoint, and we miss much in doing so. They confront their problems at ground level, using their noses mostly and their eyes only little, as they work literally at grass-roots.

Detecting where a running pheasant has gone, or where a rabbit may be in its seat (and almost scentless), or the many other questions which occur every shooting day, is undercover work. A human opinion on it is almost always worse than useless, unless based on actual observation. It is their world, not ours, and we do well to leave them to it. But we do not do well if we fail to estimate accurately the degree to which game sense is possessed by whatever dog we happen to be shooting over. It is a quality absorbed in varying extents by different dogs, and in varying forms by different breeds.

137

Allowances have been made for this in the manner by which we handle our dogs – when we command them in efforts to help them, and when we refrain.

Because they have to find all the game twice – first to flush, then to retrieve – spaniels need a double dose of game sense. Here the capacity to absorb training, as distinct from self-learning, can be made counter-productive by unimaginative handling. Within the limits of essential discipline, any gundog must be allowed latitude to use its own initiative; more reliance must be placed on the dog's memory and self-discipline, less on control.

The complicating factor is that initiative will develop only with time, after enough situations have arisen for a dog to recognise them and, without human intervention, employ the tactics which it has successfully used in the past. If, by then, too rigid a disciplinary framework has been established, scope for initiative may have been denied to the dog. This seems a more immediate risk with springers than with cockers. Observe the differences in attitude, springers being always optimistic, and cockers being realists with no inflated opinion of the human race.

A springer, *lieued* into cover empty of game, will enter with a merry noise of cracking branches and snapping twigs, emerging only when the emptiness has been confirmed beyond doubt. A cocker, having formed its own estimate of the prospects with uncanny correctness well in advance, does not often disguise its contempt for any such proposal. A pitying look for its master and a perfunctory inspection is a normal response. Men have grown grey in the effort of kicking out such places in attempts to prove their cockers wrong (myself among them), seldom with success.

A properly trained springer, stopped and given new directions when runner-hunting, will cheerfully comply – being the optimist he is. No matter what his education, a cocker's look back at his master is apt to be eloquence itself in such circumstances. 'Why are you blowing your whistle, you tedious fellow,' it clearly says, 'I am at grips with the problem, not you; just leave me to it.' The cocker will then press on, regardless of the intervention, with whatever it was already doing. The fact remains that, more probably because of this than despite it, cockers are among the most successful of all runner-getters.

It is in working a rabbit in brambles or whins, which connoisseurs regard as among the supreme expressions of spaniel work, that the growth of applied memory over the years most clearly reveals itself. A young spaniel and a rabbit are in the same patch. The spaniel is determined that the rabbit shall emerge; the rabbit is determined otherwise. The ensuing commotion may last several minutes, to the entertainment of bystanders, before the rabbit bolts. Two seasons later the same dog will have his rabbit in the open in half the time, more often than not breaking cover towards his Gun.

The skills which cannot be taught to a dog can be, and are, self-learned by dogs of the right breeding which have not been brain-washed. Breed and function determine what skills are to be thus acquired.

Labradors become especially clever at so casting themselves as to have the wind coming to them across the target area, when a marked bird has fallen in roots or a similar crop. In contrast, flatcoated retrievers have to learn to do the opposite. Their habit is to take too much wind. Trial and error teach them to move confidently into the wind towards a mark, or to a handler's indication. Assessment of scent by pointers and setters provides a particularly interesting example of a self-acquired skill. Some of these dogs learn very rapidly the hazards of questing too fast, and of taking in too much ground on a bad-scenting day. Pointers and (despite a reputation for impetuosity) Gordon setters often have two styles – a free-going one for normal conditions, and a cautious one when scent or wind is catchy. English setters, the bird dog counterpart of English springers as the optimists of their group, are more reluctant to engage low gear in difficult conditions.

Most familiar of all is the self-acquired skill of carrying a hare. When gripped across the back at the point of balance and held high, the rigidity of the hare's spine supports its weight, enabling the dog to move freely beneath the load. A dog can discover this only by retrieving a number of hares, lighting accidentally on the proper method, and remembering how much easier it made the job. In East Anglia, where hares are numerous, few top-class retrieving dogs go through their first season without picking up the knack. But where covert shooting is the norm, and hares less often met, it becomes the hallmark of the grizzled veteran.

Having reviewed the inherent and mental characteristics internal to gundogs, we may now see their effect on some familiar points of difficulty in training and management.

PART III

IN PRACTICE

12

FORMS OF RESTRAINT

Since the objective of training is that a gundog shall fulfil its own inborn instincts in a manner subordinate to its handler's wishes, any artificial restraint countervails the main aim. Prevention and compulsion are direct opposites of the volunteer spirit, and therefore wrong in principle; moreover the means by which both can be effected are difficult or impossible under the conditions in which men and dogs operate in shooting. The cover which dogs are required to penetrate, and the distances at which they work, both preclude any physical link with their handlers. Equally obviously, a man carrying a gun and perhaps a game bag across rough country does not wish also to have a dog on his hands. Therefore the extent to which restraints are useful is limited to that of aids in training.

Even in that their use is subject to a further restriction. Anything which compels a dog's compliance must at some stage be discontinued, and a dog would be quite exceptionally stupid if he did not take note of the presence or absence of the restrictive factor and, in its absence, take full advantage of freedom from it. Nevertheless there are uses in training for artificial or fortuitous restrictions of which the slip or lead is the most obvious example.

It is a matter of common observation that those who possess the worst-behaved gundogs are among the most reluctant to put them on the slip, preferring to make the welkin ring and empty the surrounding area of game by shouting loudly, angrily and often ineffectively. In contrast, those who possess the best-behaved gundogs, including the leading professional trainers, lose no time in putting their dogs on the slip as soon as there is no reason for them to be free. The conclusion is that much of the misbehaviour of dogs on shoot days is caused by misuse of the slip (or lead) in public and at home. The rights and wrongs of attachment deserve study.

To clarify definitions, a slip is a self-contained running noose; a lead is swivelled to a collar. Collars should not be worn by gundogs for safety reasons (the risk of a dog being hung up in heavy cover being self-evident) and it is taken for granted that no trained gundog would be allowed to run free on a public road, so the slip only will be referred to henceforth. It cannot be assumed that all gundog owners or their attendants (including those to whom they are married) know how to put a slip on a dog correctly.

The proper way is for the hand end to pass over the dog's neck. The noose attachment then lies below the dog's right ear, unless the owner is left-handed and so, when carrying a gun, leads his dog on his own right side, in which case it will be under the dog's left ear. If the slip is put on in this manner the effect will be that when it tightens pressure will be applied at the points where it is most effective and also the most humane. If the slip is put on the other way round the effect can be described in one word, 'negligible'.

For trained dogs my preference is for the simplest of cord slips. They fold small in the pocket, and it matters little if they are lost. For young dogs which have not yet learned to walk composedly on slip, a choke-chain is recommended. Severity should not be deduced from this. The reverse is the case. A choke chain, properly used, is much kinder to the dog and is analogous to a double bridle on a horse. Each keeps the animal collected with minimum effort if the human partner has 'hands' – which implies not only reflex dexterity, but sympathetic imagination too. The effect on a dog is greatly to reduce the incidence of disunity with its handler, and to render correction more decisive with less effort and consequently less stress from rebuke, and strained temper in the handler. Here I am not referring to young puppies. Heel-work is one of the last things I teach to a dog, normally in the first half of its yearling life, because I wish to avoid any limitation of its initiative during the preceding months of its development. By the time it has had some experience of advanced training and perhaps of work to the gun, it is no longer empty-headed, having outlived the constant wish to dash away unbidden and play around, so heel-work generally develops more or less of its own accord. Nevertheless, since a gundog should always walk on a loose lead, and the indignity of owners being taken for walks by their dogs seems widespread, the technique of applying counter-measure by choke chain deserves mention.

With the dog to the handler's left and the choke-chain correctly worn, the slip is held in the right hand at about the height of the handler's lower chest. The slip should hang without tension if the dog walks in its proper station at the handler's knee, tightening itself only if the dog begins to move ahead. When such movement changes in effect from tightening to actual pulling, the hand holding the slip is cut away sharply rightwards and downwards, closing the noose abruptly round the dog's neck, releasing the tension immediately. The action must be decisive, not tentative, the aim being to make a positive impression on the dog. To injure a dog by doing this is impossible short of gross misinterpretation, and the great virtue of the choke-chain over other forms of slip is that the noose collapses instantly when pressure ceases, eliminating all element of strangulation.

Imposition of sudden, short pressure from this particular angle has a remarkable effect – why, I cannot say. The dog's usual reaction is to look round at the handler in awe and wonder, never having experienced such a sensation before. Most dogs will begin pulling again a minute or so later, perhaps to establish whether the previous reaction could be repeated, or whether the handler achieved a mere fluke. On discovering that it can be, most dogs forthwith become total abstainers from pulling.

This small ploy, valuable as it is in freeing humanity from the misery of being towed about, is an infinitesimal fraction of the wider role of the slip. To think of its use as no more than a restrictive practice is a big mistake, but some people seem to go through life oblivious of the slip's constructive value psychologically as well as physically. Others apparently see cause for pride in not using a slip at all. Observe two extremes in human attitudes.

'The trouble is,' says an exasperated Gun, huffing and puffing, fumbling and cursing in his efforts to get his dog on to its moorings, 'he never sees a slip at home. He's all right when he's not excited, so we don't have to bother to put one on.' Bystanders can form their own opinion whether, on the evidence before them, this policy has much to commend it. Even at home those who know their stuff invariably have a slip available when a dog is out of its kennel. Their attitude expresses the difference between the positive and negative effect of the slip.

A slip is not merely a means of restraint to be used when all else has failed. To see it in this way is tantamount to regarding handcuffs as the foundation of moral rectitude. Perhaps no more revealing a measure of dogmanship exists than the mere act of putting a dog on slip. It tells the observer more about the man than about the dog. Where the process consists of grabbing, fumbling and strong words, only the negative side of the slip is known to either man or dog. How different when all that is necessary is to hold the noose and click the tongue for the dog willingly to put its head in. There the positive side is revealed as being known to both.

For a properly trained dog, to be put on slip is like a homecoming. It is a sign of duty done, combining reunion with its handler and the order to march at ease. Until the slip is next removed the dog is at rest. It can switch off the effort of maintaining self-control. The handler is in total charge, the dog off-watch. To vary the metaphor, the slip is a neutral gear for a trained gundog. To a gundog not yet fully trained, it has the further valuable effect of affording the handler a way of temporarily taking the mental pressure off the dog during instruction as well as ensuring its safety at other times.

So the slip's influence emerges as the semi-opposite of what it is often taken to be. Physically, it is a restraint; psychologically, and more importantly, it can and should be a release. Since this undoubtedly becomes established in the minds of well-trained gundogs, the moment of return to slip being clearly pleasurable to them, the converse must be equally capable of being established. This is that the moment of being unslipped is the moment for the dog to re-start behaving itself. Its off-duty period is ended; self-control reactivated; the dog must act responsibly again.

Even in training, it is customary to avoid physical restraints although able trainers of the past tethered their dogs for certain lessons in steadiness. Personally I would do so only as a last resort, for reasons already stated. But it is surely preferable to 'anchor' an unsteady but otherwise useful dog when shooting driven game than to allow it to run in, and annoy other people. There are several useful designs of anchor available, and in the interests of the peace of mind of the rest of the party they are to be recommended. Better to bear cheerfully the slight embarrassment of being seen to use one, than to endure the major embarrassment of one's dog becoming – and perhaps being openly declared – a public nuisance.

Most trainers of pointing dogs find the check cord, thirty to forty yards long, indispensable at some stages of training, such as teaching the turn to whistle. They, of course, require to teach their dogs actions and reactions to be performed at a distance; moreover they operate on open ground. Trainers of retrievers and spaniels are able to teach the correct response to commands and situations at close quarters; and their dogs, ultimately, must perform them in cover. The difference in the use of the check cord is total. Considerable skill of hand is necessary in either case, but on open ground the line does not become snagged. In cover it does so repeatedly. To keep the essential uninterrupted 'feel' between handler and dog is virtually impossible when bushes are being continually lassoed, and in my experience a check cord is a counsel of despair with spaniels, and was never necessary with retrievers.

A training line is much more practical in spaniel training. It should be as light as possible, consistent with being strong enough to hold a dog, and about six feet long. The dog is allowed to wear it, trailing behind, until its presence is forgotten. To me its main use is in countering that irritating phase through which most English springers go when learning to retrieve, of returning to the handler and then, at the last moment, jinking round him. A foot on the line, or a quick pick up, soon convinces the would-be humourists among puppies that evasion is impossible, funny joke though it would be if it could be made to succeed. The easement which the training line affords the handler has the advantage of enabling him not only to assert his superiority, but to do so in the effortless manner which most impresses young dogs still reluctant to accept a human as their pack leader.

The most essential of all artificial restrains except the slip is, of course, the rabbit pen – in suitably small doses. If it is big enough, has sufficient cover, and is stocked with wild rabbits, it is invaluable and sometimes irreplaceable for teaching steadiness to fur. But after three visits only the dimmest of dogs fails to realise when it is in a rabbit pen, and when it is not. Unless great care is taken, two standards of behaviour develop, and the trainer finds himself with a dog which is rock steady in the pen, and far from steady outside it. I have found that the preventive for this situation is that a session in the pen should be immediately followed by actual work to the gun on the nearest rabbits outside it. The lessons of the pen will not have faded and, if they are then defied, the pen is available for corrective measures.

For such situations as this fortuitous restraints should never be ignored, but noted and stored in the memory bank. Netted lanes on pig farms, rabbit-netted forestry plantings, enclosures temporarily bounded by electrified sheep braiding, angles of walls, even a tennis court, all provide enclosure or semi-enclosed environments on which to straighten out a training problem with a dog which must be prevented from escaping. If all goes well the impossibility of its doing so should not be allowed to dawn on the dog; by keeping it as an element of surprise the trainer's status as a superior being is again enhanced.

13

THE WHISTLER AND HIS DOG

The whistle is co-equal with the slip as the only two essential aids in gundog work. The word can mean the sound itself, or the instrument which produces it. Here we are concerned with both, but primarily with the instrument, because the details of its employment lie outside the scope of this book.

To dispose of the gloom first, the best and the worst of the whistle will forthwith be faced. The best of it is that the whistle is much the most useful audible link between man and dog. It far transcends the human voice in range, effectiveness and non-excitability. The whistle to a dog handler is as the rein to the horseman, his first and most acceptable channel of communication; without it he feels helpless, and may indeed be helpless. It is the sonic expression of himself. It becomes in time almost part of him, an appendage invested with accumulated powers of luck and fate, something in which he puts such faith that it develops a kind of magic.

The worst of it is that the whistle therefore becomes regarded as a kind of totem. It is blamed when things go wrong by handlers who are themselves at fault, camouflaging from them the real nature of whatever shortcomings there are. Some of those for whom their gundogs can do no right expend much energy in considering the supposed merits of different whistles, trying first one and then another in a vain attempt to rectify failures which belong elsewhere. Of course it is a human privilege for the man who is falling short of his objective to blame the inanimate instruments of his pursuit. We have a saying about the workman and his tools. The golfer who is not holing out buys a new putter instead of lining his shots better; the shooter who misses changes his gun instead of holding straighter. And the handler whose dog does not stop when he blows is tempted to buy a new whistle, perhaps one new whistle after another.

In fact, the possibility exists that he may just be right. But even if he is correctly identifying a change of whistle as a need to be met, it is by no means certain that he will change to the right one. There are many different types of whistle on the market, or made to measure by whistle addicts for whistle addicts. In estimating what faith to put in the chosen specimen it will help to consider first whistles in general as if they were part of the dog, and then to examine half a dozen examples as case histories.

Looking at the matter from the viewpoint of a handler who is having trouble (we all have trouble sooner or later, and until we do we can keep relatively calm about whistles), the temptation is to suppose that a dog which will not obey the current whistle will be more likely to obey a louder one. This is far from being true, for two reasons. First, it may well be that what needs to be increased is the receptivity of the dog, not the power of the whistle. Secondly, since loud sounds have a confusing effect on a dog, it may equally well be that what is needed by the dog in question is a softer toned whistle with a less disruptive effect.

Unless a dog is physically deaf, we may well wonder at how small a sound it can hear, provided it wants to hear it. So the first consideration in relating whistles to failures in co-operation is to consider the dog's mental attitude to its handler. Does the handler have his respect? Has the dog a sincere wish to serve him? If the answer to these questions is 'No', the whistle is not yet made which will of itself turn them into 'Yes'; and until they are turned into 'Yes' there will be no effective control, via whistle or anything else, by that man over that dog. The whistle can attract only a pre-existing wish by the dog; it cannot compel the dog itself, or alter its will.

My dogs are kennelled in a barn adjacent to the house. No matter how softly I tread, I cannot walk in soft slippers along the intervening passage without hearing them stir and jump out of their straw beds to rattle the kennel gates in hope of action. The smallest sibilance is command enough for a dog which is waiting for that sibilance, eager to respond. We therefore arrive at the point where we must ask ourselves not only, 'Does the dog need a different whistle?' but also, 'Might it need a softer one?'

My limited experience has taught me that not all dogs react equally well to the same whistle, and that it is necessary to find and use the whistle which suits each dog. This is a nuisance, because from time to time, it compels me to carry and work with more than one instrument, when I much prefer to keep my aids to a minimum. Nevertheless I accept the necessity, just as I accept the necessity to vary my tone of voice according to whether the puppy I am training is bold or timid. Some whistles are evidently oppressive to the canine ear – not always those which one would expect to be so – others are persuasive. It is evident that a dog's aural sensitivity differs from ours, quite apart from their ability to hear tones too high for us to register.

The best whistle of all is a natural one, produced through one's own lips or teeth and rendering unnecessary the use of any artefact. My own version of this, though unimpressive, is good enough to keep my dogs with me at home or when shooting over them. The difficulty is that if I am under tension, as when in company with strangers or competing in a field trial, the knack of producing it is apt to desert me at critical moments. I gather that I am far from being alone in this. Nevertheless, for those with sufficient talent one's self-produced whistle is greatly to be preferred. I suspect that the thinner sibilance of a tooth whistle is more successful than the rounder note of a lip whistle.

Some professionals recommend a pea-whistle. This need not be blown very hard, but the vibrancy resulting from the agitation of the pea is held to have some arresting quality. For shock effect the rounded metal whistle used by football referees, or the straight-barrelled gunmetal design which used to be issued to the police, are in a class by themselves. They have never appealed to me, partly because I do not enjoy loud noises, especially in the peace of the countryside, and partly because the siren which immobilises strong men at Twickenham and similar places would surely empty the countryside of game. Of course, things are not always what they seem, but I prefer to avoid the risk.

A traditional design for experienced gundog men is the so-styled Acme Silent Whistle. This is made of metal, with adjustable pitch, and is not in fact silent to me although some other people do not hear it. 'Are you actually making some sort of noise with that thing, or merely looking important?' asked a fellow Gun one day as I blew an Acme to recall a retriever long gone on a runner. He was in healthy middle age, did not claim to be hard of hearing, yet did not hear what I heard – a twittering similar to a bosun's pipe. I have found the Acme well-suited to retrievers. They pick up that little sound a great way off, turning smartly to it at quarter of a mile and more, and at closer ranges work happily to it, too. Not so spaniels.

Spaniels, of course, work closer to us, or so we hope, and from them the Acme has more often than not drawn a different reaction which I can only described as daunted. Tails have gone down, ears have dropped, the sparkle has drained away; occasionally a backward glance asked, 'What have I done wrong?' as if, instead of blowing the small note of a silent whistle, I had harshly administered a rebuke. From that I deduce that to the sensitive though ardent spaniel temperament the silent whistle is a severe command; too severe for many of them.

My favourite whistle for spaniels, in use for years, is of stag's horn (the brow point of a royal, to be precise). It is the simplest of all whistles, depending for its note entirely on the cutting of the step. The same design also works well in wood and plastic. They have the great advantage of flexibility of tone and volume, so that the user can 'play' them in the manner best suited to each dog and to the occasion – a soft message for the highly strung, a chirrup for a faintheart, a peremptory reminder to the headstrong. And I have never known it produce the adverse effect, already described, little short of resentment, which resulted from inadvertent overstressing with a silent whistle.

From this I deduce, though no expert in the matter, that the canine ear finds empathy in the lower frequencies, and that some canine ears recoil from high frequencies. Significantly, the soft note of a hunting horn has a low frequency. So also has a type of whistle latterly increasingly popular with some professionals, and especially with lady handlers of golden retrievers. This, basically similar to the stag's horn and its derivatives, has a round, fruity, almost bassoon-like note of a solemnity which almost proclaims it as a communications channel for retrievers, rather than for the mercurial spaniels.

Despite the need to find the type of whistle which best suits each dog – or even the individual whistle because, of those made of stag's horn or wood, no two are identical – one thing remains strange but true. A dog seems able to recognise the blower of the whistle as readily as it distinguishes the whistle itself. It must happen more often than not in shooting that two or more people simultaneously work dogs to apparently indistinguishable whistles, but cases of genuine confusion on the part of the dogs are very rare. In field trials, where the smallest incident is seen, monitored and discussed by a well-informed assembly, similar whistles are very frequently used by several competitors; indeed, in the case of the widely popular Acme, facsimile whistles.

Only once have I felt myself the victim of circumstance through that cause. It happened that two of our retrievers were running in the same stake, the other being handled by my wife. At one stage we were under the judges together and, as luck can be relied upon to have it, working at the same time on different birds at opposite ends of the line. We were both using Acmes. The young bitch which I handled, having picked her bird, heard my wife's whistle in the distance and set off towards it. I eventually stopped and turned her – by that time a very mystified figure – and took her retrieve which she somewhat doubtfully offered me. She had, of course, heard my wife use her Acme innumerable times at home. Evidently we all have our mannerisms on the whistle, of whatever type, which makes our individual whistling style unmistakable to the dogs which work for us, no matter how many other retrievers are being blown in the vicinity. A dog's ear, like a dog's eye, is almost instantaneous in picking up something familiar or something strange in the sight or sound pattern.

Apart from its effective range, a whistle's great advantage is that it is less likely than voice to convey to the dog any anxiety, uncertainty, anger or other stress which the handler feels, and would do better if kept to himself. But of course it is not a perfect disguise for the emotions; nothing can be. At a trial it often happens that a group of spectators outside a wood, following the unseen action within by analysing the sound effects, will detect a note of agitation in the whistling and remark, 'So-and-so's in trouble.' Be sure that so-and-so's dog became similarly aware much earlier. Although a whistle can and should be made eloquent, its successful use depends on the eloquence being kept under control. Urgency, prohibition, and encouragement can all be usefully transmitted at their proper moments; their inadvertent transmission at other moments is far from useful. The whistler must keep an ear open for his own performance, and never stop thinking of its effect on the dog.

Another form of eloquence is to be carefully avoided. This is the mixture of vocal and whistle messages. Often the vocal element consists of as much comment as guidance. The sequence will not be unfamiliar: Whistle . . . No response . . . 'Come in, damn and blast you' . . . Whistle . . . No response.

It is improbable that the dog has failed to hear all this. It is certain that it has not been taken seriously. The change from one sound-medium to another has the effect of separating the messages, destroying whatever accumulated messages the whistling might be building up without substituting a clear command to replace it. A man saying 'Damn and blast you' cannot thereby persuade a dog that he expects compliance – not because of the words used but because a man would not use such words unless he were in some degree off-poise, a fact which he cannot conceal if he speaks. The dog will then be off-poise too, and unity between them will not be regained until both calm down. The foundation of man–dog communication is concentration and avoidance of distraction. To switch from one language to another, which is what mixing whistle and voice means to a dog, cannot do anything except distract. Trust the whistle.

14

Noises Off

Other forms of noise, the inadvertent kinds, loom larger in a dog's life than some people think. They loom large, too, in the lives of their owners; so large that noise often comes to be regarded as a nuisance factor only. Its significance to the health, mental attitude and performance of working dogs is consequently ignored. The adverse effect of uncontrolled noise can be great, and seldom greater than in the vital, unrepeatable months of a gundog's life in which it is learning its job, or should be. Then the pliancy of its developing mind is best maintained by elimination of all distractions, and freedom from every unnecessary strain.

For practical purposes, we are concerned with noise in two forms. First, the noise which dogs themselves make; secondly, with the incidental noises of the world around them. Both can be a source of stress, sometimes enough to prevent absorption of training. Those concerned with any form of high performance livestock – racehorse trainers, dairy farmers and Hunt servants could all testify – become well aware of the value of tranquillity. Disturbance means energy-expenditure, which goes counter to speed, stamina, productivity and mental awareness. Gundogs are no different from these examples. Therefore consider noise.

It is undeniable that the dog, when allowed to be so, is one of the world's noisiest animals. If there is any doubt on the point, human neighbours will soon dispel it in the case of anybody who keeps a habit-barking dog in a populated area. But human neighbours are not the only sufferers. The kennel mates of barking dogs, even those which are themselves barking in imitation, suffer as a result of the noise and associated restlessness around them. There is no need for this to happen. Prevention lies in a combination of discipline and management.

Dogs bark for different reasons at different stages of their lives. It is normal for the young of any species, including our own, to create unnecessary noise; perhaps to make their mark upon their surroundings by telling the world they exist, perhaps as challenge and response in some of the acting-out games which are part of growing up. In other words, puppies bark because they are puppies and not much can be done about it except to give them something else to think about. In due course, their training will itself provide that something else, and the interest it arouses in them is the most effective prophylactic against the mindless, continuous and maddening barking which is the worst thing that dogs can inflict on man, and which may become irremediable when the dog is adult.

The cause of it lies chiefly in lack of occupation, especially when this is compounded by loneliness. A solitary dog with nothing to do, perhaps lacking experience with which to occupy its mind, is a ready candidate for the role of obsessional barker. It cannot be blamed. Only a change in its circumstances will cure it. And at least barking is seldom a nuisance where more than one dog is kept.

It may be argued that plurality is not in itself a sure prevention for barking. Cases do arise where two dogs bark twice as much as one; sometimes a whole kennel bark persistently in chorus. In these cases two things are beyond doubt. One is that the management, not the dogs, is to blame; the other that all the dogs are being subjected to enough disturbance-stress to undermine the performance of any that are being seriously trained. Continuous barking is not natural to adult dogs, which normally bark only in response to stimulus. But barking can become an addiction and, once the habit is formed, an addictive barker may well become a barker for life.

Discontent is fundamental to excessive barking. Left to themselves in peace and comfort, most dogs will settle down to that calm existence which comes naturally when life makes no demands on them. Gundogs are more ready than most to do this. Labradors excepted, they have no very strong guarding instinct; their hunting instinct replaces it in those breeds which are spaniel or setter based. My own dogs make no secret of their belief that, when bedded down for the night, they are off duty until morning. Late callers are not barked at; indeed we could have been murdered in our beds without their voices being raised, though the house terrier would sound the alarm. I regard this lack of vigilance as being some sort of tribute to the manner in which our gundogs are kept. It is practical without being luxurious, being designed to give them what they need while insulating them from what they should not be called upon to endure, and evidently succeeds in making them carefree.

Working dogs need good food. If well fed they can enjoy (and enjoy is the word) their next most important need, which is sleep, provided they have comfort and warmth. Comfort is provided by cleanliness, warmth is provided by themselves. Dogs require no artificial heat, provided they are dry, free from draughts, and clean. Given these three provisos their clear eyes, shining coats, high spirits, contentment and evident well-being in sub-zero temperatures never cease to amaze me. But the well-being is real, and depends on avoidance of insomnia. It is the sleepless dog which barks, and the ill-kept dog which loses condition in hard weather.

Coat parasites keep a dog awake. The deep sleep which it needs as recovery from effort is reduced into a series of cat-naps. In the intervals of scratching it barks. It does likewise when cold. Lack of a place in which to lie snug leaves it discontented; denied the chance of peaceful rest, it barks in frustration. Stand by an open window on the first frosty night in autumn, and note which of the neighbourhood's dogs are persistently barking. They will not be those which are decently and considerately housed. The frequent mistake of overcrowding multiplies every other contribution to restlessness. Too many dogs for the space available exaggerate territorial problems; even wild dogs have their sense of propriety and privacy expressed in terms of how many a cave will hold.

Young dogs growing up in an ambience of raised voices – canine as well as human – and sometimes angry voices have a much reduced chance of achieving the confident, sensible outlook which comes of a background which, in their manner, amounts to a happy home. At the same time all dogs must come to terms with noise, learning to separate from its pervasive background those sounds which are significant to it. Too insulated an upbringing presents its own and different problems.

In our era of aircraft noise, traffic noise and crowds, excess of silence would seem an unlikely problem. It is a fact, however, that many gundog puppies have difficulty in adjusting to the casual sounds of normal life, simply because their upbringing has been carefully organised to give them maximum peace and quiet. The transition is not often one which presents prolonged difficulty, provided it is recognised as existing. Exposure to noise has two obvious effects on a dog until toleration of it is built up, tiredness and confusion. For seven years our spaniels travelled to Scotland each August in the guard's van of Motorail. Despite being in the immediately familiar surroundings of their own boxes, they were evidently below par, showing diminished alertness in response to orders for thirty-six hours after arrival – two nights and the intervening day. No amount of work which they were subsequently called upon to do would produce a comparable lassitude.

To make noise familiar, all that is necessary is to behave with a little calculated carelessness. Doors should not always be carefully closed; an occasional bang, just often enough to be taken as a matter of course, soon wears out the element of surprise. The clanking of buckets, which it is hardly necessary to stage-manage in any household which includes pony-orientated daughters, serves an especially useful purpose. It enables dogs to become accustomed to metallic sounds.

Metal noise, as we shall see, has an especially disturbing effect on dogs. Their experience of it began comparatively late in their evolutionary chain, and the spell of the unexpected seems still to exist. The distant sound of a beetle knocking in stakes causes no alarm among the dogs within earshot; nor does the noise of rubble being tipped for hard-core. Both would have been everyday industrial noises as far back as the Old Stone Age, and dogs no longer need to learn to live with them. But strike one hammer blow on a piece of angle-iron, and every dog within a furlong radius will bark energetically at what seems to be regarded as a sinister intrusion. If a dog can be made steady to metal-on-metal a long stride has been taken towards noise toleration, and towards self-control in the presence of disturbing noise, and eventually towards its own noise-control. The effort is worth making. Noise in its several ways is a curse on the man–dog relationship.

15

GAME AND GUN

All the more because of their intuitions about their purpose in life, the minds of gundogs are not shock-proof when first they meet the two entities which loom larger than all else in their world. Each encounter produces a moment which may have to be managed with sensitivity and understanding lest the impression it creates goes wrong. These moments are those in which a young dog first holds in its mouth newly killed game, and when for the first time it becomes fully conscious of the gun. It is evident that both these experiences, when what has been a formless excitement switched on by casually encountered game scent suddenly becomes real, have an effect which can temporarily arrest the processes of the brain.

Game with the life not long gone from it still has the feel of a quarry, lacking only its vibrancies; the smell of it is the smell of that enticing but unseen source of scent encountered often but not requited until now; its taste will include a hint of blood, a single pellet wound being enough to release that disturbing influence. For a young dog to have such an object in its mouth, in close proximity to nose and tongue, to be carrying or holding it, becomes traumatic in the literal sense, having the quality of a dream which suddenly and unexpectedly comes true. All the stirrings of inherent consciousness, all the unexplained surges of exhilaration when game scent has been met, are suddenly reawakened and confirmed in this instant of fulfilment. It is enough to obliterate all else from the wondering, inexperienced mind of a puppy, and it very often does.

Hence the need for special care in taking from a puppy this, its first freshly shot retrieve, even if proficiency on cold game is complete. It will, of course, have been easy work; there must be no risk of failure, hence no complications. The puppy will have gone out to the marked fall, as it has done so often to dummy or cold bird, and picked it up as a matter of course. But then, finding itself overwhelmed by the medley of sensations released by scent and taste and feel, it returns with its mind blanked out.

What often happens is that the puppy comes back to its handler as if all were normal, sits, holds up the bird or rabbit to be taken in exemplary manner, but then retains a firm hold on it, apparently refusing to deliver. It is possible to become exasperated at this stage. Everything has gone well. From weeks of work with dummies or cold game the puppy has learned to give up gracefully whatever it brings in. Its present conduct has all the hall-marks of a sharp attack of stupidity, and in essence is indeed that. But to treat it as such will do no good, and may do positive harm in making the puppy temporarily a shy retriever, or the irreparable harm of making it hard-mouthed.

All that has happened is that in the strange magic of the moment – compounded of surprise, delectation and triumph – the puppy's mind has been so filled with new realisations that it has forgotten to open its mouth. It will need to be helped, and the help must be given in the gentlest possible manner, so that the puppy is unaware of it and takes the eventual delivery to be the consequence of its own actions. Opening the mouth except to take something into it is an unusual action for any animal, and especially for a carnivore. The chain of communication along the nervous ganglions is therefore far from automatic, requires to be positively activated, and is certainly not a reflex when all the puppy's perceptions are reeling in a state of pleasurable shock. This fraught moment may recur several times. Whenever it does, the puppy must be helped again with unvarying gentle-ness until the time comes when it yields its jaw of its own accord, as it will with patience.

The other first encounter raises the dread possibility of eventual gun-shyness, that bitter disappointment which seems so much more frequent than it ought to be. Dread possibility? Perhaps the word is misplaced, because it seems to me that many owners of gundogs do not dread it enough. Casual acquaintances point to the retriever or spaniel destined to live out his days at home on a hearth rug, and say something like, 'I'm sorry to say he's gun-shy. Don't know why. With his breeding he should be all right. Too many Field Trial Champions behind him, I expect. Some of them are very highly strung, I think.'

The words quoted verbatim are characteristic of many. They reflect the misconceptions that if anything is wrong with a gundog it is not the owner's fault, and that a gundog's pedigree is a specification of what it will do, as distinct from what it can do. In consequence the dog is regarded as a thing, like a car, as distinct from a being, like me or its owner. We learn to confront many varied situations as we go through life, and the capacity to do so is to some extent dependent on the character our ancestors bequeath us, and to an equal extent on being taught how to. So with a gundog. It may, in modern terms, 'have what it takes' as a result of parental influence. Whether it can use 'what it takes' is a matter for whoever is in charge of its development. It is also a matter on which to proceed with the outmost caution, in the realisation that failure, if it occurs, will almost certainly be in the human element.

An inherently and irreversibly gun-shy dog is most exceedingly rare. But the possibility of allowing gun-shyness to develop always exist. Mismanagement can and does turn this possibility into fact, and a familiar pattern of attitudes which bring it about can be quoted as a cause, though not the only cause.

Perhaps it is a sweeping generalisation, but gun-shy dogs seem apt to belong to very confident men. He whose dog has this problem often seems at first sight too much the breezy optimist to have any problems whatever of his own. On reflection a deeper truth begins to dawn. Since the two conditions may well be related, sweeping generalisations must now be abandoned and my own experience, slight as it is, be considered less as an example than as a point of departure for others. One relevant element must first be made clear: nobody in his right mind could conceivably describe me as a breezy optimist, especially on this subject.

Ever since I first trained gundogs the spectre of gun-shyness has haunted me. Tales of woe on the subject were never lacking. However, it is a fact that, even including the neurotic retriever which was my sole total failure, I have never had a gun-shy dog. I believe the reason to be the healthy state of trepidation in which I approach introduction to the gun. This has existed, indeed has grown, since I realised after training three or four dogs that the problem, though much feared, had not yet arisen for me. There had to be a first time, I told myself, determining to postpone it as long as possible. One day, no doubt, it will happen. But meanwhile I have held it at bay longer than some.

As a defence mechanism, I regard every dog as potentially gun-shy. Though I believe the definitively gun-shy dog is rare, I know that dogs which are initially nervous of the gun are not. Among English springers I have found them a majority. Even among dogs which are not gun-nervous there are many, perhaps a majority, which could be made gun-shy, given enough thoughtlessness.

Whether a dog shows signs of nerves or not, I treat all alike. But while allowing for their possible apprehensions, it is important not to be soft with them; such an indication of apprehensiveness on one's own part would be as counter-productive as the opposite extreme – unbelievable, and yet met – of assuming, as some men do, that if a dog is nervous of shots, their constant repetition will make it tolerate them.

Far too much is taken for granted in the relationship of dogs and guns. 'It is their nature to tolerate gunfire, so they will'; such is the faith of those who, unless they are very lucky, are heading for a gun-shy dog. There is very much more to the matter than that, and I believe in being on the safe side.

In the first place, a conviction strengthens in my mind that in the canine mind the presence of the gun and the powers of the gun are separate, and a young dog should be brought to accept them in two stages. My method is to begin my performing gun-like actions with the thumb-stick which I always carry – bringing it to the present, the port and the slope, swinging it as if on to a bird, as well as just waving it about, until the stick ceases to possess any element of surprise. It should not be necessary to add that no dog in my care has ever been struck with a stick.

Then, one day, instead of a stick I carry a gun – and with it go through the motions to which the dog has become accustomed when done with a stick. In addition I break it and close the breech several times. Eventually, accidentally on purpose so to speak, I lay the gun down so that the dog can go and smell it, and of its own volition by very easy stages begin its approach to the moment of truth.

This it invariably does with great interest and concentration, which should never be broken by speaking or moving. The different scents given off by metal, wood, oil, and residual gunpowder are presumably all analysed. In a surprisingly large number of cases their cumulative effect is to arouse a curiosity, almost a mesmeric attraction – and this before the dog has had any chance to know what a gun is for, what it can do, and the part it will play in his life.

When once the gun is thus accepted as something familiar, the effect of the noise it makes seems the more easily managed by common sense. The first gunshot is at a distance (not 'over' the dog as seems to have happened, unsurprisingly, in some cases which have not gone well), the distance being progressively reduced. The avoidance of echo – trees and steep hillsides being as effective echo-producers as buildings – is essential. A single shot is tolerated but a double shot, near enough simultaneous to sound like a single to human ears, has an unnerving effect. I once saw a five-year-old and very experienced labrador cower uncharacteristically when a trigger defect caused his master to fire both barrels inadvertently a micro-second apart. And a close-up echo is as near a parallel to a double shot as can be described.

The whole process of gun-indoctrination, from stick introduction to toleration of shot, takes me about two months. It is conducted low-key, as if it did not matter, at a dosage-rate of not more than twice a week. One pertinent underlying factor is that the dog has not led a quiet life, for reasons stated in the preceding chapter. But familiarisation with noise merely removes an obstacle to familiarisation with the gun. It does not achieve it. I am strongly persuaded that it is the gun itself – the mystique and awe of this alien if attractive object – which first unsettles a dog's nerves, and leaves it vulnerable to the sound it makes. Reassurance does not necessarily come naturally. It must be arranged. But it is not needed if a preliminary course is given in gun-familiarisation.

16

GUIDED MISSILES

The points have been made that the degree to which a dog will control itself in accordance with its handler's wishes is proportionate to the respect in which it holds that particular handler, and that respect is dependent on the dog's estimate of the handler's infallibility. Make no mistake, dogs, especially gundogs, are not saintly. Though a dog will behave as one reasonable being to another with a handler it respects, steps will be taken at intervals to try the handler out and determine whether he continues to be entitled to respect. A reputation for infallibility, like all other assets, needs care and maintenance. The price of it is eternal vigilance.

To say that a reputation for infallibility rests in the handler himself, not in the mind of the dog, may seem to stress the obvious. Nevertheless, a surprising number of shooting men, finding that a dog is getting a bit above itself, send it to a professional trainer to be 'straightened out', and believe the problem to be thereupon solved, which is not altogether so. This is undoubtedly a wise course if, and only if, the limits of what can be achieved are understood and accepted.

The trainer can make the dog obey him, and will probably do so without much trouble. But he cannot make the dog obey his owner when returned to him if the owner proves vulnerable to insubordination when the dog carries out routine exercises in 'trying it on', which he can be relied upon to do. The trainer will have re-established in the dog's mind the principle of obedience. The owner alone can turn that principle into habit by establishing his own infallibility. The greatest barrier to infallibility is distance. Every bright gundog knows, or thinks it knows, when it is out of range of authority. The man who can undermine its assurance in that regard has gone a long way to establishing his own infallibility and thus perpetuating the dog's respect.

To do this he needs the further reputation of ubiquity, the capability of being everywhere. If the dog feels that no matter what the apparent distance between them, his handler is always in touch, in the literal sense of being to make a contact, he will mind his 'p's and q's' wherever he may be. To him it is as if his handler possessed infinitely extendable arms, or a magical knack of being twenty yards nearer than the dog had supposed. Such a man or woman becomes, in its mind, capable of anything, hence not to be underestimated.

In creating this desirable illusion one of the most under-employed of aids is the simple one of missiles. To have the right things in one's pocket when exercising a dog, and to be mentally and physically prepared to use them, saves trouble in the long run. It is important to remember that missiles are not recommended as a means of dealing with emergencies, but to establish an ascendancy of man over dog so that emergencies do not arise. Take, for example, response to the whistle as the disciplinary detail through which pressure can be exerted to achieve all-round smartening-up.

In over-simplified terms, the principle may be put thus. If the dog ignores the whistle, throw something at it. The questions of why, what, and how must have been answered in advance of the trainer's mind if the result is not to be harm rather than good. The underlying factors are that a signal to a dog, in whatever form, must be regarded by both the sender and receiver as an order, not a request. If an order is ignored, something must be done about it.

The worst thing to do is to repeat the order in the form in which it has already been given. If it has not been obeyed the first time, there is no reason to suppose that it will be obeyed the second time. The end-product of repetition is to prolong indiscipline, and eventually to perpetuate it. What is needed is a means of calling the dog's attention to the fact that a command has not been carried out. It is probable that the dog is already aware of this, but sees no urgent need to vary its agenda and so continues what it was already doing, such as blowing down a vole's burrow. This is hardly consistent with respect for its handler, and suggests an unflattering human parallel. We have all seen the dog which, when called, responds with a look which well embodies the traditional civil service assurance that 'the matter is under active review' (which may actually mean that the functionary responsible is about to retire, and will pass the buck to his successor). We expect better of a dog.

Action must therefore be taken to convince the dog that its human partner is not a conveniently remote and relatively immobile figure, incapable of action outside a limited radius, but on the contrary is omnipresent. So the missile comes into action as a contact-maker, not as a piece of weaponry or as a means of retribution. Its repeated employment causes the missile to become accepted by the dog rather as a tap on the shoulder from an arm of the law, with the injunction 'You've had your order, now get cracking'. It is

163

not to be regarded as punitive or as a shock tactic. Either would be counter-productive, quite apart from ethical considerations. Its sole purpose is to persuade the dog that higher authority is never out of touch.

Therefore the trainer who goes out without, so to speak, a shot in his locker is one degree worse off than he who goes out without a lead on which the dog can be put if emergency demands. Worse off, because emergencies do not always arise, whereas slow responses certainly do; if they did not, dogs would not require training.

If a moment comes in which the only sensible course is to throw something, and nothing else is available, the traditional advice is to take off one's boot and throw that. I saw this done, by an eminent Irish trainer. His expertise was impressive. He snatched off his boot and threw it in one smooth action, projecting it far and accurately, with a fast arm as they say nowadays, and finished teetering impressively on one leg, in the manner of one who had just put the shot. The stance was made necessary by boggy ground. There he remained, heron-like, until good order was restored. The dog was equally impressed. It returned in a hurry, full of apologies, and was promptly sent back to retrieve the boot. The incident was an object lesson in various ways.

Those who do not wish to perform the feats of this difficulty with their boots must provide themselves with alternatives. These must be of the size, nature and substance which cannot injure the dog, and should possess rudimentary ballistic qualities. My own preferences are for small apples or chat potatoes in my pocket. Both have the disadvantage that those which miss are apt to be picked up and either retrieved with a humiliating air of sang-froid by the dog, or eaten, to the detriment of the final law enforcement. This does not happen to those which score hits, since they bounce off the dog's body and are lost, the surprise of the unexpected contact preventing the dog from marking them. Accuracy is therefore essential, and must be acquired.

Those who can throw down the wicket from thirty yards nine times out of ten have no difficulty in this respect. Others should practise. Some, my wife among them, use catapults projecting soft objects such as those I throw. So does a young friend more recently attuned to this device than I. For those caught unprepared and lacking a missile, I highly recommend clods of earth. They break on impact, cannot be pursued or retrieved, nor cause harm. Their disadvantage is that they are difficult to throw accurately, or far.

Two cautionary points deserve mention. Missiles should never be used when more than one dog is running free. Those not concerned in the measures being taken will in all probability run-in, to the risk of their own morals, to retrieve whatever was thrown. The original offender will then join in the fun, consequently forgetting that he was in bad odour, and what was intended to be an inculcation of brisk and orderly compliance ends on a note of low farce. No word should be spoken at any stage. One syllable of the human voice can obliterate the memory of the contact, or undermine its significance. Even when correction has been effected, absolution should be given by touch of hand alone.

17

CRIME AND PUNISHMENT

The truth about a difficult and emotive branch of the subject will be faced as bluntly as possible. We live in a soft society, much softer and much more riddled with major and minor crime – including violence – than that in which many of us grew up. The opinion that miscreants of the human race should suffer for their offences, if expressed, regularly alarms those day-dreamers who will not recognise reality. So even the thought of punishing a dog is enough to cause sentimentalists disquiet. But it has to be done.

Nobody in his right mind enjoys doing it, any more than surgeons enjoy amputating legs; but that, too, has to be done when circumstances compel it. We who train dogs must look upon the subject of punishment in precisely that light. Not only the punishment itself, but the necessity for it, are matters of regret. We would be happier if neither had happened. We all harbour the private feeling that the fact of their happening is a reflection on our competence as trainers, and very often there is substance in this.

However a situation in which punishment is the only recourse is not one for moralising, but for action. More is likely to be at stake than the working competence or competitive excellence of the dog. Its own future perhaps, its own safety very often, and to some degree the safety of human beings – always in some degree subject to accident when firearms are being carried – may well be threatened if a particular defiance is not corrected. The central practical question is 'How?'

It would be easy to disguise the answer under some of the routine euphemisms, for experts do not readily come down to brass tacks on this issue. We are told, for instance, that 'stronger measures may become necessary' (to quote only one recent example) but not what the stronger measures are. I shall be more specific.

Assuming that the trainer has satisfied himself – not merely beyond reasonable doubt, but beyond any doubt whatever – that an order has been defied and that the dog knows it, punishment is the unavoidable remedy. It is advisable to move slowly towards this conclusion, so that the trainer's mind may be clear, before the definitive offence is next committed, on what this course of action is to be, for he must take it promptly, decisively, and above all calmly when the moment comes. My own self-rule is never to punish for a first offence, but only for an aggravated repetition. It is better not to punish at all, if this be possible; a distinction must always be maintained between mistakes and crimes; there may be a mitigating circumstance; or some other circumstance may threaten to dissociate the dog's mind from the misdeed which earned the punishment. If none of these escape clauses apply, then sentence must be carried out.

Since punishment is something to be avoided if possible, the most desirable sequel to it is that it should not require to be repeated. Therefore the prime essential is that it should be severe enough to make an impression which is both immediate and lasting. This will not be achieved by being half-hearted. Better no punishment at all than punishment which falls short of its intended effect. To that extent, the end must justify the means. But the calculation cannot be dismissed in such rough-and-ready terms.

The concept of 'making an impression' has two applications – physical discomfort and mental realignment. The former presents the fewer problems. Punishment must always be so designed as to avoid injury and a dog very soon, sometimes all too soon, recovers from any elements of ordeal which it may undergo. So what matters is not what happens to the dog, but what the dogs thinks of it – in short, the mental impression. This is likely to be rather different from what ours would be in such a situation.

The idea of subservience to authority is commonplace in Nature, in the wild as much as in domestication. The pack leader, be it wolf or dog; the dairy herd boss cow; the first hen in the pecking order; the chief of a red deer herd, generally an old hind past breeding age; the master starling in a flock of thousands; the dominant horse in a paddock, again generally female. Toeing the line by animals does not originate with the human conception. Evolution prepared the minds of many species for it, much further back in time, and present generations are well prepared for it.

Therefore the worst thing that can result from punishment, the opposite of the best thing already referred to, is that the punishment should not be severe enough. The consequence of under-doing retribution is to leave the dog with a disdain for its trainer which it would not acquire in any other way. Those who mete out physical punishment, and fail to make a thorough job of it, invite a very understandable reaction from animals whose toleration of suffering is, by our standards, enormous. 'If that's the best he can do,' the dog seems to reason, 'I can take it any time. To blazes with him and his orders.' And a rebel is thereby created, instead of quelled.

167

For me, physical discipline is largely an uncharted area. Whenever possible, therefore, I seek to make my impression more directly on the mind. In this process the trainer has a valuable and negotiable asset in the confidence, even love, which the dog has come to place in him. I prefer to work on that, inflicting upon the dog's faith in me the contrasting elements of humiliation and contempt, to the other method of inflicting pain on the dog's body. This preference is dictated by the practical consideration that I have no way of knowing how much pain is necessary, nor do I have much confidence in my ability to lay it on appropriately. Nevertheless, whichever approach we prefer, the out-turn of events will dictate that we must apply both on a some-and-some basis, and we must be prepared to do this.

Fond as I am of them, no evidence has come my way that dogs have a moral sense which enables them to distinguish between right and wrong. What they do have is the capacity to distinguish on the basis of experience which sequence of actions will be approved by the boss class for whom they work (us) and which will not. I do not know whether my attitude is softer than average and, if it is, my practice of giving the dog the benefit of every reasonable doubt does not result from any nobility of character but from the practical realisation that if a fault results from a failure in communication, physical punishment is not the most promising way to make communication more certain in future.

Given that the element of defiance is identifiable (we can all recognise it, since we encounter it often enough) my objective is to make a mark on the dog's consciousness which will secure compliance in future without reducing its confidence in me. This is explicitly different from letting off steam or bolstering my outraged ego.

In the process I put no great faith in anything which involves striking the animal. Dogs do not beat each other. When the pack leader quells insubordination he seizes the offender by the lip, the ear or the throat, more rarely by the scruff or the foreleg, and gives it a good shaking. This is the manner in which canine domination is exercised, and I do likewise.

A dog thus grasped by a man is at once in a position of inferiority. If lifted clear of the ground (i.e. parted from its natural element) inferiority is intensified into subservience, embarrassment, even ridicule of which dogs are sharply conscious. A shaking, demonstrating that anything a dog can do, man can do better, is all that is needed to underline human superiority. This superiority will be related to the offence if it is imposed exactly where the offence occurred, without delay, without anger (though obviously with indications of disapproval) and above all without an intervening act of obedience by the dog, however small.

To those who feel they lack the confidence or the strength to lift a gundog and shake it, I would add that it sounds more difficult than it is. My physique is not impressive, and I am not young, but springer spaniels give me no problems. It is ten years since I treated retrievers similarly, but the meal sacks which I lift and carry as a matter of course (though admittedly do not shake) weigh twice as much as a labrador, and I would foresee no problems.

But obviously there are ladies and others for whom, for one reason or another, this procedure would be impossible. For them a whip or its equivalent, which for me is a very subsidiary option, may be the only course. I use such a thing less as a punitive instrument than for its shock effect, and because being pliable it cannot cause injury. My version of a whip is a worn-out motor-car fan belt. This has the advantage that it can easily be carried concealed, and used with the advantage of surprise. One wordless clip down the quarter of a dog which walks ahead when it should be at knee generally lasts a lifetime.

The degree of punishment depends not only on its severity, but on its duration. A dog, when put in its place by another, indicates surrender by rolling on its back and the incident is forthwith closed. The victor sees nothing to be gained by prolonging the ordeal of the defeated, which leads me to believe that there is nothing to be so gained by us. Pain and fright confuse any animal's mind, and to continue retribution beyond the point at which a dog can any longer remember clearly the events which gave rise to it is not only senseless but counter-productive.

Two sharply effective lashes with a fan belt is the most I ever give. I emphasise that they are wholehearted. When I pick up a dog and shake it, a sincere attempt to dislodge its back teeth is continued for a maximum of five seconds. Then follows a vital component of any corrective measure, reconciliation.

Some experts advise that an erring dog, having been 'straightened out', should then be left alone in its kennel 'to think things over'. With respect, I disagree, not having found this helpful. Nor, on reflection, would I expect to. What has happened is a failure of communication, of confidence, or of will-power. Whichever has been lacking, it should surely be restored by contact sooner rather than later.

Any physical measures being ended, the psychological *status quo* must be re-established. I put the dog on the drop, stare down at it for a few moments silently and with as much contempt as I can register, and then walk away twenty yards or so. For five minutes I relax and admire the view, looking towards the dog but not at it. Then I walk back to it. There is no need to make a fuss. Whatever is my habitual greeting-contact, a touch on an ear of a pat on the chest, is enough. Then, the incident closed but not forgotten, we walk away together as friends.

From this it may be inferred that a trainer needs to be something of an actor. Indeed he does. To convey the sense of contempt by voice and eye-expression is a valuable technique to master. The dog knows, instinctively and immediately, when human regard turns from warm friendship to chill disapproval. Cold contempt, a clear freezing of the relationship, can visibly deflate a dog, and in producing that effect there should be no mercy. Psychological pressure is as effective, if not more effective, than physical pressure and must be applied with that knowledge in mind. Hence the vital nature of the eventual forgiveness.

The reconciliation is not mere sentiment. It has a practical effect in sealing off the episode, becoming a kind of bulkhead between the before and the after. Until the reconciliation a dog will do all in his power to ingratiate himself, and win back the favour of his partner. If he is allowed to succeed he will, in his own mind, have imposed his will and thereby the dog will have emerged the winner. Reconciliation, offered and given effect by the man, denies this initiative to the dog. Thereafter he will have no need to ingratiate himself, no way of turning his humiliation into a victory.

The chief aspect of the actor's art through all this process will be the trainer's concealment of his true feelings. His attitude must be clinical, even glacial. On no account must he display anger, even momentarily and acci-dentally. Anger may (though rarely) be displayed for a purpose, but it has no purpose here. Anger implies caring; and caring is inconsistent with contempt and, by giving its object some degree of importance, counteracts humiliation. A dog, of course, does not know these psychological complexi-ties, but it can sense the drift which underlies them. Anger, after all, is a form of fellow feeling between whoever feels it and whoever causes it. Dogs crave fellow feeling with their masters; perhaps for this reason they at times behave in a manner to promote anger, because anger is better than nothing. And for them the worst form of nothing is to be shut out, in spirit, from a master who is leaving no doubt that he has ceased to care – until, of course, he himself indicates differently.

In human affairs we think much of making the punishment fit the crime. In dealing with dogs the need is different, being to make the punishment apply to the crime. The dog must be in no doubt what it is being punished for, and in establishing this, its greatly developed sense of locality is the main aid. If a dog has offended it should be taken to the exact position where the offence was committed, right to the precise buttercup off which it moved without permission when left on the drop. Not all crimes are so conveniently committed as that example.

Take the familiar instance of the young dog which, having ignored a turn whistle, goes self-hunting. There is little that the handler can do about it, except protect himself from subsequent misunderstanding. If he stays where he is, and the dog returns to him in that position, he will be precluded from any disciplinary action, even expressing displeasure, because the dog will then be doing what it ought to do, in short committing a legal act, and thereby placing itself beyond reach of blame though unquestionably guilty. The handler must put the dog in the wrong. He does this by going after the dog, not in any hope of catching it, but with the aim of meeting it before it can return to the handler's original position. He must if possible be moving towards the dog when they meet, and should contrive to do so in a menacing, even doom-laden, manner. He is then in a position of moral superiority, and can exploit it.

Punishment must be kept simple in cause and effect. The dog must know, afterwards as well as before, for what the punishment has been administered. Hence it should be done in silence, to avoid the confusion attendant on remonstrance in more than one medium at a time. The handler's manner should be sharply different from that which he adopts in training sessions, to prevent punishment becoming mistakenly associated with instruction. And though the whole object of punishment is to mark the memory, it must not scar it.

18

WIND AND LIMB

The energy demands of gundog work vary widely. It has been calculated that a foxhound covers about forty miles in an ordinary day's hunting in which the field might have had, if they were lucky, two quick things of twenty-five minutes each and a point up to three or four miles. In a day's rough-shooting a good-going springer spaniel must travel not much less. To be on the safe side let two-thirds be assumed, say twenty-five miles, virtually all of which will have been in cover. The resources called up from comparatively small bodies are in proportion enormous.

By contrast a retriever, walking at heel or sitting at stands and working only after drives, has an almost pedestrian, sometimes sedentary occupation punctuated by intermittent sharp bursts of activity. Its energy expenditure, compared with that of a spaniel, is much less. Both, and perhaps the foxhound, too, are greatly exceeded by pointing dogs which, questing a two-hundred-yard beat for several hours on moorland, must achieve a truly formidable mileage over country which is often very testing. This is especially true of Irish setters in their native land, where dogs often work all day on thinly populated ground with miles between the coveys. The stamina and endless keenness of these lightly framed dogs of wiry physique have to be seen to be believed.

All gundogs however, retrievers not less than others, need to be fit to the extent that the stresses of their normal work can be withstood unnoticed throughout a normal day. Well-managed dogs of working strain in any of the four gundog categories are well capable of this, though by no means all gundogs seen out at shoots show signs of being well managed. Some all too evidently blow hard after little exertion, and to the knowledgeable eye some of those which are superficially up to their work are suffering from lack of complete fitness. But since it is virtually impossible to tire a gundog to the point of its being unable to continue working in some fashion, it may be asked why the raising of its fitness to a degree closer to athleticism should be desirable.

The reason lies in the demands made by the canine mind on the energies available in the canine body. It is an often-confirmed saying that a gundog's mind, including the perceptory senses, tires *before* its body does, losing its sharp edges of awareness and promptitude of reaction. Uncharacteristic mishaps may then occur – a running pheasant is not collected which should have been, a seated rabbit is missed, a bird dog blunders into a covey and flushes out of shot. The truth of the matter is less generally recognised, and this is that the mind tires *because* the body does, but before the tiring of the body becomes apparent.

Therefore the maintenance of gundogs in the state which the old-timers described as 'hard meat' – up on their feet, firm in muscle, clean of wind, filling their skins, and bright of eye – is operationally important and not just a fad. The proposition really equates with the old tag so beloved of school-masters, a sound mind in a healthy body. In a day filled with physical activity, varied situations, fast action, the former is impossible without the latter and can become crucial when some sudden exceptional test has to be faced – a high fence to jump when carrying a heavy bird or a hare, or a long swim on a cold day against a strongly flowing river.

The balancing of energy output and input is obviously fundamental to physical efficiency. Food must always be related to the amount of activity needed at the time. High living is essential for gundogs in the shooting season and for the month or so of recovery time which follows it. But it is not necessary during the summer when body heat does not require to be maintained and energy expenditure is minimal. An overload to be carried for the early months of the succeeding season is the inescapable consequence of failure to adjust after the preceding one.

In the basic management task of keeping dogs in a condition to their work both well and easily, two fallacies have done great harm for generations past. One is the supposition that exercise will remove surplus weight; it will, but if exercise alone is relied upon to do this, the strain imposed upon the dog's constitution will almost certainly cause lasting harm, and the dog's later life will prove it; to reduce the food intake is the most sensible, economic, and humane remedy for a thick-winded, corpulent dog. The other fallacy is the equally familiar half truth that a healthy dog is always hungry; it is, but a hungry dog is not always healthy.

Since it must be a gundog owner's aim to have health of mind as well as of body, forethought is needed during the half of the year when the activi-ties for which gundogs live are suspended. Their days must not become dulled by unvaried routine. They need to be kept thinking, their responses maintained at active service sharpness. Elements of surprise can be worked

173

out and implemented. What seems in anticipation to be an uneventful, even boring, period can be made exceedingly interesting. It is a time for reappraisal in which there is much to do and to be observed, a time when truth dawns – on, for instance, physical soundness, which is taken for granted during the months of work.

Too often, failures in this respect are not the result of the passing years, of fair wear and tear, but of the degeneration which can result from modern attitudes and artificialities. A springer spaniel's sight may be going. Two forms of inherited blindness afflict the breed. Or a labrador may have advancing hip trouble. That, too, is inherited. In spite, indeed in a way because, of modern science, such troubles have grown more widespread in recent years.

The dogs themselves are not to blame. Their fate was decided on the day of their parents' mating. Nor are most of their owners to blame, though perhaps they should have known rather more about the bloodlines (and some of the Champions) in the pedigrees when they bought their dogs as puppies. So, indeed should the breeders themselves, except that inheritance is debatable, and hindsight easier than foresight. I believe that most blame attaches very clearly to trends of the age we live in, and not only to show-breeding.

Long-term harm results from the modern obsession with rearing every puppy in a litter (including those which Nature would have put down), often at considerable cost to the breeder, and even greater cost to the eventual owner. The causes include plain sentiment, the over-valuation by breeders of their own bloodlines, financial considerations, and ill-judged motivations which are sometimes aided and abetted by vets. The result is that culling, essential to the maintenance (let alone the improvement) of all high-performance livestock, no longer happens. None of us like to put down puppies. We all hope, even if we do not quite believe, that every litter contains a champion-to-be, and naturally fear that whelp which is ailing may have the stuff of greatness in its small body. To lose a puppy when £10 each was the price was less of a blow than it is nowadays when a £500 cheque is the size of the gap that is left.

Many vets see in their professional ethic an obligation to save life if they can, as in the rearing of sickly puppies. One can respect this, even while reflecting that the livelihood of vets depends on an adequate supply of defective livestock. More serious is the incidence of unstable temperaments at a time when it is not rare to hear the owner of a difficult bitch claim to have been advised to breed a litter from her 'to steady her down'. If there is a better way to populate the country with unreliable dogs I have yet to learn of it.

The biology of the female dog is such that it is capable of producing, twice a year, several times as many puppies as are necessary to amortise the death rate for its species. This was Nature's way of subjecting the species to selection by survival of the fittest through enforced culling. We negate that culling, as we are in fact doing, at our peril, no matter how supposedly high minded the reasons for obstructing natural selection.

19

REST AND RECREATION

Rest is as essential for our dogs as it is for us if form is to be maintained for strenuous activities involving the brain as well as the body. By rest the resources depleted by effort are replenished and made ready for more effort. If more effort ceases to be required, as when the close season for shooting brings a stand-easy to all gundogs, recreation provides a healthy outlet, and it is to be hoped a constructive one, for energies which have been re-built. When one or more days of shooting a week are keeping gundogs busy, most of them past the puppy stage work out their own design for living, generally sleeping contentedly between one expedition and the next. They can sleep on with advantage for another month when sport has ended. But thereafter they need a degree of organisation if the benefits of rest are to be developed by recreation into a freshening-up process. If this does not happen, the opposite will; the effect of the long lay-off will be deterioration in the mental reflexes, however well their physical needs have been met.

Generalisations abound on what to do with gundogs in the close season. As usual, the conventional wisdom on the matter tends to contradict itself. Compare the following undoubted truths:

Few things do a dog more good than a quiet spell in kennel, where it can rest, calm down, and emerge refreshed. But few things do a dog more harm than boredom, which can leave it frustrated by cessation of activity, feeling neglected and without sense of purpose.

Nothing succeeds like retrieving in giving a dog activity and keeping it aware of its subservience. Nor does anything succeed like too much retrieving in making the dog uninterested.

Obviously some activities are necessary. The form they take must be calculated to avoid excess of any one of them, to maintain the zest for living usefully, and to keep the man–dog relationship so firm that when, months hence, the next day's game-shooting comes round, neither party is 'green'.

Consider the outlook of each.

After the last day's formal shooting ended in a January dusk, most

176

experienced dogs which had been at work all season were probably happy enough to find themselves warm and dry in a straw bed, listening to rain hissing down outside through the mainly uninviting days of February. There would be occasional pigeon shoots, at which the services of a gundog are seldom essential, and even then not strenuous. Some might be lucky enough to have occasional and more exhilarating hours at rabbits. That first interlude, soon to end as the pheasants begin laying, therefore presents few problems. But life begins again in April, and so does the make-or-break period for gundogs.

Initially, the human view is probably similar. Only when fair weather comes, and despite the seasonal urgencies of farm and garden, does realisation dawn that something ought to be done with the dogs. But what? With confidence, I offer another generalisation. The foundation of high performance out shooting, and still more in competition, lies in the home or the kennel, whichever the dog chiefly inhabits. It is impossible to put a dog into neutral. Daily he will be renewing his opinion of his master. It is essential that this renewal should take the form of an enhanced regard, not an adverse modification. Therefore a code of conduct is as essential, perhaps more so, for owners as for dogs if the impression each forms of the other is not to deteriorate.

One impression which the dogs must not form is that the owner is their servant, not their employer. This can easily happen, especially to conscientious owners who rightly make a practice of personally feeding their dogs. It is difficult for dogs to look with the right degree of disciplined attention on one who has allowed himself to become, in their eyes, more of a waiter than anything else. Rather than allowing himself to assume this identity, with the consequent need eventually to shed it and emerge again in the aura of leadership, an owner must contrive to appear in more commanding guise. By deed, never by pretence, his image must be that of the most significant and interesting feature of the whole scene – so that it may continue as such when guns are firing, game flushing and falling, and hares going away in full view.

How this is done is a matter of each man for himself. All that is common to everybody is the ultimate object, the manner in which we wish our dogs to see us. It is not enough that they should look on us with affection, though affection is the basis of all. It must, however, remain consolidated into respect. The right relationship, in which the dog can always trust the man and the man can always trust the dog, is not achieved by contact with any such concept as the dog's better nature. It has not got one. We owners can work only on the nature it does have, which is an animal nature, canine not human. It is compounded of qualities which include basic instinct, hunting instincts, self-preservation, the capacity for fixating on another being, curiosity, long memory, sensitivity to experience, alert senses, rudimentary reasoning power and extended depths of loyalty and generosity.

At home my own close season aim is to imprint on these attributes a sense of shared interest, leading to mutual confidence. Outside, I throw some dummies, walk-up some hares for steadiness' sake, hunt gorse and bracken for rabbits, do disappearing acts behind trees and hedges, and in other ways keep myself watched and wondered at. It is not what is done, but the way in which it is done that matters. The end-product is that a good time should be had by all, regularly until the guns come out again. Then the first day of the new season will not be a return to another world, but just one more situation with which a well maintained team spirit is able to cope.

Such a pattern has its element of variety, but can hardly be called strenuous. I make no apology, for I do not share the popular supposition that dogs 'need exercise'. They get exercise – in plenty, as we have seen – when they are doing their life's work. They enjoy exercise, except in hot weather. But they actually need very little exercise of the fabricated kind laid on for their benefit in the form of 'walks' which, if they have no wider aim than locomotion, do gundogs as much harm as good.

More nonsense is talked about exercise for dogs than about most subjects. The real purpose of exercising gundogs is to keep them healthy outside their working season, only secondarily to make them fit for the next season. This is quite separate from the further consideration, which is generally the governing one, of giving their new owner the self-satisfaction of feeling that he has done his duty in performing a routine largely irrelevant to the animals' welfare.

Assuming adequate stock-sense in its housing and feeding, how much exercise is enough to keep a dog in physical health? Enough to keep its feet from collapsing, and to stimulate internal functions. But, it may reasonably be asked, how much is that? Obviously dogs vary, but the requirement can be surprisingly little, and I can call as witness a Glen of Imaal terrier employed in my home as house guard and court jester. This little-known breed, originally bred for badger-digging, much resemble greatly magnified weasels. To the hand ours is hard, muscled-up and carries no spare flesh. Eight years old at the time of writing, she has decided her own regime since puppyhood.

She takes what most people would regard as exercise at intervals of eleven months, being a determined abstainer from all such concepts as 'walks' except in Scotland. When taken out on a lead, if only the quarter-mile to the Post Office, she had to be towed against her determined resistance every yard

178

of the outward journey, which was very exhausting for whoever took her (so the time soon came when, to her great satisfaction, nobody did). Her normal daily programme has been to accompany me on fine days, if necessary breaking into a trot, while I feed the home-based livestock, a round trip of perhaps two hundred yards. After this she loses no time in re-occupying the warmest corner of the kitchen, remaining there until evening feeding time, her own included. If the weather be wet or cold, she has always needed to be physically evicted if she is to enter the outer world at all.

Every fourth day or so she does two or three circuits of the lawns at a flat gallop, during which the wise bystander keeps well clear; she has neither the intention nor the ability to stop or swerve and, weighing about 45lb, is no light matter in collision. After this performance she shakes herself, wags her tail, and dives back for warmth and comfort. It is my conviction that she knows exactly how much exercise she needs, and that is it. No healthier, brighter dog could be imagined. On each first day of our annual month in Scotland she participates in the family pipe-opener over anything between Ben Rinnes and Lochnagar, covering probably twenty miles when all rabbit reconnaissances are included. Despite the idle months behind her, she shows no sign of fatigue, only eagerness for the next day's ploy.

Of course a gundog needs more close season exercise than this, but not much more, and not often. What we know as 'exercise' is more valued by the dog for the opportunity it gives for being in its owner's company than for any effect on its health. For proof of this, examine the belief that if a dog is 'let out' it will exercise itself beneficially. It will not. In enclosed ground a retriever finds a warm spot, lies down, and waits for something to happen. A spaniel digs a deep hole where no hole should be. To 'let out' dogs on to unenclosed ground is an excellent way of teaching sheep-worrying or self-hunting.

A further belief without much foundation is that a dog's return to full working fitness is necessarily a major operation, like conditioning a hunter. It is certainly 'major' in the sense that it has to be done. But as the physical make-up of different life-forms vary, and as the transition rate for dogs is rapid, whether improving or retrogressing, the process of getting a dog back to form is not a long one, provided it has not been allowed to become fat. For a human athlete to pass from mere well-being to peak performance at middle-distance takes a year. For a horse to come from grass to full racing fitness takes six months. For a gundog to harden up from rest to working condition is easily accomplished in a month. Provided it has been sensibly managed, two or three partridge days are enough.

Dogs do not deteriorate in kennel if the kennel is large enough, if they are

179

not neglected and therefore bored, and if their feeding is adjusted proportionately to the non-expenditure of effort. A flabby dog with the shambling gait which comes of pasterns collapsing under excessive weight is the product of mismanagement, not of lack of exercise. Owners do themselves a good turn when they divert their own energies from the exercise fetish into other ways of keeping gundogs interested, more relevant to their work, and for which mere bodily activity is not enough.

One aspect of rest and stress which is easily overlooked is that of transit. There are two viewpoints on it, those of the dogs and those of their human fellow travellers. Gundogs are not small. They are active, enterprising, fit and strong, apt to be tired and wet or muddy at the end of a day, and plural rather than singular. Transporting them in comfort but without inconvenience raises different problems from those presented by a single household pet.

Assuming an estate car or hatchback, the two most usual methods are a dog barrier or a travelling box. Barriers have the advantage of neatness, and the disadvantage of vulnerability; boxes the advantage of space-saving, more positive restraint, and more restful travel for the dogs, offset by the disadvantage that nearly every make of car calls for its own extempore design. These pros and cons need amplification. Not only must dog-barriers look good and be capable of being locked into position without damage to the inside of the vehicle, but they must give security as distinct from merely appearing secure. This is less easy than it may seem. It is part of the job of spaniels and retrievers to surmount or penetrate obstacles. They should be as capable of doing so as commando soldiers, and most of them are. If it is to be effective when needed, a barrier must have a deterrent capability as nearly as possible like the perimeter fence at Colditz.

Nothing less is enough because the term 'when needed' does not indicate periods when the car is being driven. There is small need then for a barrier of any sort, since only an elementary degree of control is needed to ensure that the dogs stay where they are put. The barrier's function begins, and it will assuredly be thoroughly tested, when the car is parked with the dogs in it, and the human occupants leave. One dog in every three will while away the ensuing idle time in breaking out. Where one leads, any others present will follow, investigating and making free with human possessions. Some, especially young and impatient labradors, can create major havoc. Most have an inexplicable zest for eating maps. One of my retrievers extended this appetite for paper to a complete set of Kennel Club Trial Rules. They did her no good.

My preference, therefore, is for a box. It is kinder to the inside of the car, kinder also to the dogs. Though some dogs, like good soldiers, sleep whenever and wherever there is no need to do anything else, most do not. Instead they watch the world go by, and in so doing deny themselves needed rest and relaxation, to the detriment of their subsequent performance. Nothing is more tiring than using the eyes.

Even if they go unremarked, the effects at a shoot are nevertheless actual. What may look like just another scatty gundog – restless, slow in response, impulsive, lacking concentration – may in fact be a very good gundog which has just sat up for fifty miles in the back of a car, wasting attention on every seemingly moving object in its field of vision, working up a thirst by panting in anticipation, becoming excited for no good purpose, and arriving physically fresh but as mentally tired as if it had already done a day's work. The critical factors in dog-box design are the car's roof height and the slope of the tail-gate. Otherwise, given adequate ventilation, the less the occupants can see the better.

Volumetric content is, of course, a doubly limiting factor. It is imposed by the size of the car, and governs the number and size of dogs carried. The latter is less of a consideration than it may seem. Some of the more gigantic strains of retriever may present problems, but the neater working types of springer spaniel, labrador and golden retriever are space economical, and even the taller flatcoat folds up surprisingly small.

20

FULL CIRCLE

For all of us, each of our dogs represents a decade of our lives. Even if we own several, or many, dogs this is equally true. A complete turn-over of those who work out their allotted span is possible only half-a-dozen times. All the more reason, therefore, to ensure that each relationship is as perfect as it can be made.

It falls into three parts – the original choice, the partnership, and the finale – and the first is the most fraught because it brings together two unknown quantities, a man who does not know the dog and a dog who does not know the man. Together they must forge their sporting and domestic future. That great decision, which dog to buy or which of a litter of puppies to keep, is one on which much excellent advice can be given but which only one man can make. Professional trainers, experienced breeders, knowledgeable friends can all say what in their opinion may be expected; but none can say, at the time that matters, how things will actually turn out.

My small contribution to the pool of wisdom is that he or she who seeks a gundog should first be perfectly clear about what sort of gundog is sought, its breed, sex, age, colour, type and character insofar as these may be predicted from its ancestors, and then let the dog do the choosing. Put the other way round, the buyer (having satisfied himself of what he wants to buy) should wait until he finds an otherwise acceptable animal which makes no secret of the fact that it has fallen in love with him. 'Like it; and if you don't like it, don't buy it' is the golden rule in all livestock deals – however good the animal is in theory, however attractive the price. A decision which may be said to be based on sentiment has also started in faith, and that is the best foundation.

That said, some things may be added about the pitfalls and priorities in buying a gundog. Pitfalls are not often the results of carelessness or folly. Generally the reason is a failure to weigh realistically all the factors of the deal. Most men aim too low. They do so for reasons of personal modesty rather than from fear of the cost of aiming higher. Price is seldom a significant factor in buying a puppy, though it certainly is significant when buying a 'male' dog. The right puppy will not be materially more expensive than the wrong one, and few men seem bothered by the initial cost anyway.

What does bother them seems to be a fear of acquiring a dog above their station, as they see it, in the sporting community. 'I don't want anything very special,' I am repeatedly told, 'just an ordinary shooting dog.' This overlooks the central reality that an ordinary shooting dog, if efficient, is indeed something very special, particularly to its owner. In extension of this, modesty extends to the estimate by would-be buyers of their own capacity to work a dog. 'I'm not an expert with dogs,' goes another refrain, 'so I don't want anything highly bred.' This suggest the curious reasoning that if a dog is lowly bred it will be easier to train and control than one with generations of successful parentage behind it.

As with most things in life, the obvious is almost always the sounder course. The man who is 'not an expert' needs a dog which is itself proportionately nearer to being one, if their combined effectiveness is to be above average. If he gives himself a real chance by obtaining a dog bred for its purpose from ancestry of proved ability in performing it, he may very soon look like an expert even if he does not actually become one. The growth of enthusiasm, which so often results when a serious effort is made to tackle the man–dog relationship, is paradoxically a major cause of disappointment. Contact with fellow enthusiasts soon exposes the limitations of a puppy bought by a man who has aimed too low. Then ambitions grow and the questions arise as to how and where to aim high enough.

This is a point on which I decline to give specific advice, except to those friends who are close enough for me to know all their relevant characteristics, including their shooting preferences and their home background. The responsibility is too great for what may amount to a bow at a venture. Reference to home background raises more issues than can be discussed here. It is, of course, crucial. But in the present context only one thing need be said, and there are many devoted husbands to whom it applies. There is only one piece of sensible advice to give the man who seeks a puppy of a particular breed because 'they do the job and my wife finds them attractive'. It is to buy her one forthwith; and then buy himself a puppy of whatever breed he himself prefers for the work he wants done. Life goes more smoothly with two dogs than with one; training is absorbed more readily by the dog for which it is top priority.

How many seasons a gundog can perform is a prime interest to all who shoot. My observation, unquantifiable, suggests that there are marked variations between breeds in this respect, golden retrievers and cocker spaniels being notably long lasters. Taking an average, perhaps seven seasons of useful performance is fairly near the truth. But this estimate raises the question, 'What is meant by performance?' At least one gallant veteran comes out in most shooting parties, a grizzled labrador or an arthritic springer perhaps. No doubt the old labrador will pick a bird or two (not too far from the peg) and the springer may flush a few that the younger and less experienced have overlooked. But such as they cannot be said to be pulling their weight, and this is not performance at normal useful standard.

Their owners watch them indulgently, remembering better days, and looking with foreboding at the shortening future. Many submit themselves to unnecessary worry over the question of a successor, fearing to bring out a younger dog in the old pensioner's lifetime for fear of causing distress. In fact, this is almost always misplaced anxiety. Gundogs who know their place in their establishments, and are aware of being trusted and valued, are seldom small-minded enough to be jealous. They lack our human frailties. The arrival on the scene of younger companions is more likely to be welcomed with pleasure by old-stagers, who forthwith re-discover their lost youth and gain a new lease of life.

But this does not alter the truth that, once over the hill, an ageing dog passes the point of usefulness on any terms except his own. We have a middle-aged cocker who understands perfectly what these terms are, and has made sure I do, also. She comes out shooting, but has ceased to be the cornerstone of the day's success, as once she was. It is accepted by both of us that I am at liberty to make any call, whistle signal or gesture I like. She will take this to apply to some other dog, to some person, even to our host; but certainly not to her. Everything in her day is optional. She will go for a bird if she sees any future in the enterprise; if not, she will go off by herself and hunt rabbits.

On arrival she assesses the weather; and sometimes, I suspect, the Guns. When the prospects do not measure up, she gets back in the car. She is therefore no longer entitled to call herself a gundog, though I would not dispute the title of consultant, as is conferred on the superannuated in other walks of life. In that capacity she can still turn in an eyecatching runner when the spirit moves her. But this is not to be relied upon. Being a gundog means being relied on; it also means day-long sustained effort, with the mind not wandering from the job in hand, wind and limb unflagging, and the will not flinching at the sight of cover or water. That kind of commitment cannot often be sustained after nine years old – seven seasons after a dog is entered to shooting at two. Even when the will is there, recurrent doubts arise over utilising it.

In an effort to identify a gundog's best years, and the degree to which form can be maintained into later ones, I analysed the age groupings of four Championship Stakes. In all cases the runners were required to qualify, so the figures represent the top level of competitive gundogs. They proved consistent. The Retriever Championship and the Spaniel Championship (in which all the competitors were English springers) each attracted thirty-two runners. In either case twenty-four of these runners (seventy-five per cent) were in the age group of three to five years. The winning retriever was a three-year-old and the winning spaniel a five-year-old. Five retrievers competed at two years old, but only one spaniel. At the other end of the age-scale only three retrievers aged more than five ran for their supreme award, one of them being the defending Champion. The spaniels produced seven similarly senior contenders – three six-year-olds, two seven-year-olds, and two eight-year-olds.

The same three-to-five-years age-group produced a majority of qualifiers in the Cocker Championship and the Champion Stake for Pointers and Setters, but by narrower margins. In cockers it produced twelve out of the twenty-two competitors, slightly more than fifty per cent, five seven-year-olds having won their way through. In the Champion Stake, for which forty-three ran, twenty-two were from the favoured age-group – fractionally over fifty per cent. Of less immediate consequence is the fact that the three-to-five age group produced the winners of all four titles. What the broader spectrum indicates is that gundogs are at their best at such ages; that thereafter the sharp edge of drive, skill and reflex begins to be dulled; that retrievers lose their competitive form a little earlier than springer spaniels, rather earlier than cocker spaniels, and much earlier than pointers and setters, of which three seven-year-olds, one eight-year-old, three nine-year-olds and one ten-year-old still had the stamina and turn of foot to survive the admittedly not over-demanding qualifying requirements.

Field trial dogs, being the athletes of the gundog community, are fitter than those which work at shooting pace need to be. The qualities which deteriorate after five years old are more likely to be those of sensitisation rather than physique. Just as an ageing golfer can still hit the ball long and straight, but finds the crucial putts no longer drop, so even a veteran gundog can go hard and bravely, but begins to miss game which earlier he would have found.

This evidence points to nine-years-old being the time of life at which proved performers become lights of other days. Thereafter progressively less can be expected of them and an easier life-style is a kindness. A successor will not be resented.

What is to happen when the realisation dawns that an elderly dog is not up to the job any more is something which exercises all our minds. The realisation, of course, dawns on the owners, not on the dogs. The dog is a classic case of the 'I'm-as-good-as-new' syndrome which is observable throughout Nature, but particularly in human affairs. The company chairman who will not retire, the ageing comedian whose timing has gone, the jockey whose nerve has worn away, the diva whose high notes exist only in memory, these and a thousand other occupational permutations are familiar to us all. Dogs are no different. But they cannot talk.

The time comes when, for dog or man, what was formerly possible is possible no longer. And the strain of trying to make it so invites the question, 'Do you think at your age it is right?' A man can answer sensibly but, again, a dog cannot. Animals have both the privilege and the handicap of being unable to imagine. Hence they cannot know that the passing years have carried away the physical efficiency which enabled them to do their work, that they are not the dogs they were, that their decline is irreversible, and that the great oblivion is growing nearer.

Without this realisation they advance towards the inevitabilities of their future without the purposeless regrets which we may feel. On the other hand, they must absorb the frustration of repeatedly failing on missions in which they expect to succeed, without knowing the reason for their failure, and perhaps of finding themselves superseded by others on those occasions which were the chief joy of their lives. Having gained so much from their companionship, we owe it to them to handle their last years or months with regard for their feelings. There can be no yardstick for the age up to which a gundog should work, other than the capabilities of the animal in question. These vary greatly.

A friend has told me of the death aged nineteen of his cocker spaniel, which had worked for ten seasons, and lived happily in retirement for seven more years. Living happily is the essence of our obligation to our dogs, and we can do much to make it possible. A cocker spaniel, a realist if ever there was one, with a selective attitude to work at any time, and a hedonist towards the good things of life, can probably adapt better than most to being on the shelf (provided the shelf is comfortable).

But to a springer spaniel, the eternal optimist with an unabating ambition to be doing what comes naturally and small interest in anything else, no such attitude seems possible. One such little old lady – frail, with the look in her eye which tells that there is not much behind it, yet trembling with eagerness – was brought to our house recently. We had bred her, and I had shot over her, years ago. She had done thirteen seasons, twelve for her then owner. He was shooting nearby, and called in while passing. He wanted us to see his heroine, and there might not be another chance. 'Whenever I send her out,' he said, 'I'm well aware she may not come back. If she does not, it's better for her that way.'

She stood on the passenger seat of his car. She cared nothing for her birth place, nor for old friends. Her questing nose vectored repeatedly to the open window, where the air stream brought the scents of rural England to the interior of the car. Her tail wagged spasmodically, as when a touch of pheasant or rabbit drifted in. 'Enough of conversation,' she was indicating, 'once more into the thick, dear friends, once more . . .' Perhaps, just once. If so, to go and not return would indeed be better for her than missing the chance.

Somewhere between these two extremes, a design for living must be found for the old stagers. The gundog has not yet come my way which would do as the veteran cocker did, and come to terms with retirement. It has been very evident that the greatest suffering I could inflict on any of our pensioners would have been to leave them at home when my gun case and stockings, not to mention the call to younger dogs, proclaimed unmistakably that I was going shooting. So, like the veteran springer, they continue to come out. The first easy bird, often the sort to be collected by hand, goes to the oldest member of the squad who will pick it with sober deliberation and then do little else all day except perhaps to lend an experienced nose to the unravelling of a strong runner's line of departure. This seems to be enough. An intelligent dog, secure in his confidence in his owner, does not become jealous of others who are given more to do.

If other owners of ageing gundogs could be similarly convinced, unhappiness might be avoided. Repeatedly people say to me that they would like a younger dog 'but the old fellow would hate it so' (referring to the senior citizen in possession). In truth, the old fellow is extremely unlikely to 'hate it'. More probably he would prove to be delighted with some young, non-human company. Introducing a puppy into a household shared by an old stager of ten or more often has the effect of taking a couple of years off the old chap's age. He, lucky fellow, does not know that he is old, although he may well appreciate that he is bored. A young companion is more likely to be welcomed as an end to boredom than resented as an interloper. Repeated cases of such rejuvenation lead me to believe it the normal reaction.

So long as an old dog, however much a light of other days, is in no pain, enjoys his food (though less of it than formerly), can move without handicap, and from time to time indicates his well-being by digging a hole, then I deem him entitled to my company until worse befalls. But when that happens, and life becomes in any way a burden to him, then I do not deem myself entitled any longer to his company, at the expense of his suffering.

It is then my responsibility that death us do part. When that moment comes, it is in my presence. We share the final experience together, as we shall have shared so many others. The important thing is that he need not know, shall not know, must not know, that there is a parting. So while the injection takes effect, and until the big sleep has merged quietly into permanent stillness, I do not withdraw my hand.

INDEX

r